WHO IS A CATHOLIC?

Who Is A Catholic?

by Richard P. McBrien

DIMENSION BOOKS
DENVILLE, NEW JERSEY

First American Edition 1971

PUBLISHED BY DIMENSION BOOKS
Denville, New Jersey

Grateful acknowledgement is hereby made to *The Catholic Transcript* of Hartford, Connecticut, for permission to use, in revised form, certain of Father McBrien's weekly syndicated columns entitled "Essays in Theology." Thanks are due also to The United States Catholic Conference of Washington, D.C., for permission to reprint some of Father McBrien's weekly "Questions and Answers" from the "Know Your Faith" series (National Catholic News Service).

CONTENTS

An Introductory Comment

I am convinced that the question posed by this book's title is a matter of considerable, direct interest for very many Catholics today, and is of indirect interest for Protestant, Anglican, and Orthodox Christians. There is clearly a crisis of identity among contemporary Catholics and I am attempting herein to offer some clarification of the various issues underlying this crisis.

It should be evident from the format of this volume that I have not intended to write a scholarly treatise in ecclesiology, nor to develop in any exhaustive manner the various topics which often exercise the minds and the emotions of many Catholics in our time: papal infallibility, the development of dogma, the meaning of ordination, and so forth. There are serious and extensive treatments of these problems already available, and I have called attention to some of this material in the bibliographical comment at the end of the book.

Instead, this is a work designed to promote and stimulate discussion among Catholics, and indeed among all Christians, on the question of the Church in general and the Catholic Church in particular. The analyses of the various issues are brief and, I hope, to the point, and the mood remains tentative throughout.

Introduction

I raise the question, Who is a Catholic?, in a manner designed to provoke discussion, not to settle it. It is not by chance that the book's title is formulated as a question and that much of the material is presented in the syntactical style of the question mark rather than the exclamation point: What is distinctive about Catholic Christianity? How is Catholic Christian faith related to the dogmatic statements of the Church? What is theology? (Although this may seem to be the most academic question of all, I am convinced that it is the most practical. A misunderstanding of the nature of theology is responsible for our common misunderstanding of the meaning of revelation, faith, doctrine, Sacred Scripture, and tradition).

What is the relationship between the normative witness of the Bible and the subsequent reflection of the post-apostolic Church? What is the magisterium? What is the scope of its responsibility and what are the limits of its function? Is there any possibility of dissent against the official, stated positions of the college of bishops, including the head and center of the college, i.e., the pope? What, indeed, is the place of the papacy in the Church?

What do we mean by infallibility and apostolic succession? What is the meaning of ordination? Should the Church at large have a voice in the selection and evaluation of its leaders? Is there any point any longer to being, becoming, or remaining a Catholic?

The table of contents provides a slightly more detailed outline of this project, and at the end of each chapter there are ample discussion questions which are designed to facilitate further probing, argument, and, it is to be hoped, clarification of issues.

Appendix I provides a sample of some of the major questions which Catholics and other Christians are asking about the present practice and experience of the Catholic Church.

The non-specialist reader of this book should not conclude that the occasionally polysyllabic discussion of Catholic identity is simply over his or her head. I did not produce this material at one sitting. The reader should at least consider the possibility of digesting it after more than one reading. If you are concerned, sensitive, and critical enough to know that some of the usual answers to the question, "Who is a Catholic?", no longer suffice, then you are the one for whom this material has been written and assembled.

Boston College
Chestnut Hill, Mass.

RICHARD P. McBRIEN

1

The Question of Catholicity

1. The Self-Understanding of the Catholic Church

Every Catholic knows that his Church has changed in the last ten years. (Well, *almost* every Catholic. That Becker Research survey taken in the Diocese of Worcester a couple of years ago still haunts us.)*

Too many Catholics, however, continue to think about these changes on a purely superficial level. They don't see any underlying theme or purpose, nor do they recognize any special pattern. The only thing they seem to understand is that we Catholics have changed many familiar and traditional practices of Catholic life.

We Catholics don't fast so much as we used to. Fridays are no longer days of abstinence from meat. The Eucharist is celebrated in our own language and the priest faces the people.

Mixed marriages can be held in church, and with a Mass. Priests and sisters are more involved in public affairs, and their activities are no longer confined primarily to the rectory, convent, or parochial school. Their style of dress, especially in the case of the sisters, has been modified considerably.

These are changes we all can see. And because we can see them so easily, we can talk about them

---

*The survey disclosed that 43% of the diocese's Catholics never heard of the Second Vatican Council.

and express our opinions about them. In the meantime, the more basic changes often go unnoticed. Too many Catholics, it seems, can't see the forest for the trees. That trite expression fits the situation exactly.

The Catholic Church is changing, to be sure, but the real changes are in her self-understanding. Because the Catholic Church has begun to understand herself in a new way, she has begun to change certain styles and patterns of her life in order to make them conform more faithfully to her new self-image.

I should suggest that the change in self-understanding has occurred, and continues to occur, at four distinct levels: (1) within the Catholic Church itself; (2) in the relationship of the Catholic Church with the other Christian churches and communities in the Body of Christ; (3) in the relationship of the Catholic Church with other religious communities; and (4) in the relationship of the Catholic Church with the world at large.

(1) The Catholic Church no longer understands itself primarily in hierarchical, clericalistic, monarchical, legalistic, and triumphalistic terms. How can we digest all these adjectives?

First, the Catholic Church, especially at the Second Vatican Council, now recognizes more surely than before that the whole Church is the People of God. This People of God shares in the threefold office of Christ himself: prophetic, priestly, and kingly. As Christ came among us to announce the coming of

God's Kingdom, to embody this Kingdom in his own life, and to bring it about in the midst of the world by his good works and especially by his sacrificial death, so too the whole Church, the People of God, is called upon to be the spokesman, the embodiment, and the facilitator of the reign of God among men.

Does this mission fall upon the hierarchy or the clergy alone? Not at all. On the contrary, the same Dogmatic Constitution on the Church states, in its fourth chapter, that "everything which has been said so far [in chapter two] concerning the People of God applies equally to the laity, religious, and clergy" (n. 30).

Is the lay apostolate simply a participation in the apostolate of the hierarchy as it was once assumed in the "Catholic Action" movement of the 1940's and 1950's? Not at all. The council insists that "the lay apostolate is a participation in the saving mission of the Church itself. Through their baptism and confirmation, all are commissioned to that apostolate by the Lord himself" (n. 33).

Thus, the Catholic Church understands more surely than before that there are no second-class Christians, nor are there any super-Christians. There are no spiritual elites; namely, the religious and the clergy. Indeed, the fifth chapter of the Dogmatic Constitution on the Church announces, in its very title, that all are called to holiness in the Church. There is no compromising with the call of Christ to

13

perfection. Every Christian must respond to that call to the highest degree that God's grace allows.

Since the Church is not composed principally of ordained officeholders, and since the mission of Christ hasn't been given only, or even primarily, to the clergy, the policy of the Church should be formulated, as far as possible, by all those who have responsibility for the work of the Church, and that means laity, religious, and clergy alike. Parish and diocesan councils are not a luxury, nor are they simply a novelty designed to keep the Catholic Church "in tune with the times." They are serious attempts to fulfill the theology and teachings of Vatican II. The Church is the responsibility of the whole People of God.

Furthermore, the Church is not some kind of super-state, with its own courts, diplomatic corps, penal system, and so forth. If it has any of these items, it must be only for the sake of its higher mission to proclaim, embody, and facilitate the coming Kingdom of God. The Church is, first and foremost, a community. It is not, in the first instance, an organization or a social institution. It is people. It is the People of God.

Nor is the Church an absolute monarchy, with the pope at the top of the pyramid. It is rather a collegial entity, which means, among other things, that it operates on the principle of shared or co-responsibility. The Church is a community composed of many local communities. Each local community, in one sense, contains the whole Church, and yet, in another sense, it is not the Church unless it is in communion with every other local community. Every pastor is the overseer or, one might even say, the bishop of his community; every bishop is the overseer of a given cluster of local communities, and he stands in their midst as a principle of unity and as a strengthener of their faith; and, finally, the pope is the overseer of the international cluster of local communities, standing in their midst, like Peter, to confirm the faith of the brethren. He is not so much at the top as he is at the center. It is not a question, in other words, of authority filtered down from pope, to bishops, to priests, to people, but of authority and responsibility given directly to the whole Church but exercised in various ways for the good of the whole body. The Church is a collegial, not a monarchical entity, the council reminds us.

Finally, the Catholic Church recognizes that it is not to be identified any longer with the Kingdom of God. The Kingdom may exist within the Church (as it must, if the Church is to be a credible community), but it is not coextensive with the Church, as if the one can simply be superimposed upon the other. As St. Augustine once said: "Many whom God has, the Church does not have; and many whom the Church has, God does not have." This means that there are many in the Kingdom of God, i.e., many people who are doing the will of God, who are not members of the Church; on the other hand, there are also many people in the Church who are not in the Kingdom of God, who are not doing the will of God. Is this really so strange a principle? Didn't the Lord himself tell us that "it is not the one who says 'Lord, Lord!' who will enter the Kingdom of heaven, but he who does the will of my Father"? The Church and the Kingdom overlap, we hope and pray, but they are not one and the same reality. The Church can never rest on its laurels and say that perfection has been given to it. On the contrary, the Church must recognize always that it embraces sinners in her bosom, that it is "at the same time holy and always in need of being purified" and therefore must "incessantly pursue the path of penance and renewal" (Dogmatic Constitution on the Church, n. 8).

(2) The Catholic Church no longer understands itself as the only viable expression of the Gospel. There are other Christian churches and/or communities within the Body of Christ. We share with them a common faith in Jesus as Lord, a common reverence for the Word of God in Sacred Scripture, and a common acceptance of the Gospel as the basis for Christian life and witness.

It had been assumed by many Catholics, until the council, that only Roman Catholics are within the Body of Christ. The impression was certainly given by some of the papal encyclicals of Pope Pius XII which said that the Roman Catholic Church and the Body of Christ are "one and the same" reality. To be a member of the Roman Catholic Church, one must acknowledge and accept the sovereignty of the pope. But since Protestants do not do so, Protestants are not really in the Body of Christ.

The Second Vatican Council almost reaffirmed that position. In article 8 of the Dogmatic Constitution on the Church, an earlier draft stated that the Body of Christ is the Roman Catholic Church. After some debate, the verb "is" was changed to "subsists in." What did this mean? It marked a broadening of our understanding of the Body of Christ. While the Roman Catholic Church does, in fact, derive its life from the Body of Christ (i.e., it "stands upon" the Body of Christ), it is not simply coextensive with the Body of Christ. There is room in the Body of Christ for other Christians who also confess the Lordship of Jesus and who wish to participate in his saving mission for the sake of God's Kingdom.

If the expression "one, true Church" is applicable at all, it is applicable to the whole Body of Christ rather than to any one community within that Body. This does not mean, however, that the Catholic Church now undersands itself as exactly on par with every other Christian community. It does not. It continues to insist that there are degrees of apostolicity and that the Catholic Church, at least in the objective order, embodies these realities to the highest degree.

(3) The Catholic Church no longer assumes that God has communicated himself to Christians alone, or to their predecessors in Israel. Rather, we have come to realize more sharply than before that everyone who calls upon the name of God, whether Christian or not, seeks to give him praise and thanksgiving and seeks to do his will in the world. Every religious community is committed in some way to the coming of the Kingdom of God. "The Catholic Church," the Second Vatican Council teaches, "rejects nothing which is true and holy in these religions . . . . The Church therefore has this exhortation for her sons: prudently and lovingly, through dialogue and collaboration with the followers of other religions, and in witness of Christian faith and life, acknowledge, preserve, and promote the spiritual and moral good found among these men, as well as the values in their society and culture" (Declaration on Non-Christian Religions, n. 2). The council says this without prejudice to its own conviction that Jesus of Nazareth is indeed "the key, the focal point, and the goal of all human history" (Pastoral Constitution on the Church in the Modern World, n. 10).

(4) The Catholic Church no longer understands its saving mission only in terms of bringing the non-churched people of the world into full communion with itself. We understand that we exist not only to

preach and to baptize, but to serve mankind in the various ways outlined so effectively in the recent social encyclicals and also in the Pastoral Constitution on the Church in the Modern World.

The Kingdom of God, in other words, is not only a matter of the conversion of the individual heart and mind to God but of the renewal and even of the recreation of the whole world through love, justice, peace, and freedom, according to God's will that we should all be one.

As the Catholic Church continues to reflect upon these basic changes in her self-understanding, she will continue to adapt and reform herself according to this self-understanding. The point of this introductory discussion is that we cannot hope to understand the individual changes without understanding the more fundamental changes in self-understanding that are going on beneath the surface.

2. *The Church: Christian and Catholic*

What is it that distinguishes the Roman Catholic communion from all other communities within the Church? The simplest, although not necessarily the best, possible response is to direct the reader to the third chapter of the Second Vatican Council's Dogmatic Constitution on the Church. Therein we can find, in conveniently synthetic form, the heart of the distinctively Roman Catholic conception of the Church.

Whereas the specific difference between Christian and non-Christian lies in the fact of baptism and the explicit confession of faith in the Lordship of Jesus Christ, the basic difference between Roman Catholicism and every other form of Christianity is its understanding of ecclesiastical office, and, more specifically, the office of the pope.

Article 18 begins with the observation that Christ instituted a variety of ministries in the Church for the nurturing and constant growth of the People of God, and that those ministers who are endowed with sacred power are "servants of their brethren." Most non-Catholic churches could accept this without much difficulty.

The council proceeds, however, to specify these ministries. Jesus established his Church by sending forth the apostles as he himself had been sent by the Father (Jn. 20:21): "He willed that their successors, namely the bishops, should be shepherds in his Church even to the consummation of the world." With the affirmation of an episcopal structure, many lower-church Protestant denominations depart from the consensus.

The final stage of disengagement is reached when the council insists: "In order that the episcopate itself might be one and undivided, he placed blessed Peter over the other apostles, and instituted in him a permanent and visible source and foundation of unity and fellowship. And all this teaching about the institution, the perpetuity, the force and reason for the sacred primacy of the Roman Pontiff and of his infallible teaching authority, this sacred synod again proposes to be firmly believed by all the faithful."

The Catholic, therefore, is one who, while recognizing the bond of unity he has with all other Christians inside the Body of Christ, is convinced that the heart and center of unity in the Church is the Eucharist and that the ministerial or hierarchical foundation of the Eucharist is the college of bishops with the pope at its head. There are degrees of incorporation in the Church, but the norm of incorporation is one's proximity to these sacramental and collegial realities.

There may, indeed, be areas for discussion, such as the precise meaning of infallibility, or the proper relationship between pope and bishops, or the theological understanding of the presence of Christ in the Eucharist, and so forth. But for the Catholic, a Church without the college of bishops, without the chief bishop as the successor of Peter, or without the Eucharist, would not be integral.

The Catholic is convinced, therefore, that the Church was never meant to be a totally unstructured "movement" or "happening." He would share the view of the Anglican New Testament scholar, Bishop John Robinson, that "it is impossible to be a biblical theologian without being a high Churchman."

21

The question that confronts the Catholic Church in our time, however, is not whether we should have a pope, or bishops, or stylized sacraments, but whether the historical development of each of these central realities does, in fact, conform to the biblical pattern, and whether there may now be room for a different kind of development.

3. How Much Change Can the Catholic Church Stand?

What sort of development is theologically possible in the Catholic Church? How much change can the Catholic Church stand?

Every Catholic would readily admit that the pope need not be an Italian. There is no argument in Scripture, history, or in the teaching of the Church that would require this. But do we also realize that the pope need not be the bishop of Rome; that he need not live in and govern the Vatican State, nor have diplomatic relations with other countries; that he need not have canonical power over all Catholics, with the right to appoint bishops, establish dioceses, etc.; that he need not wear special clothing nor be called "Your Holiness" or the "Vicar of Christ;" that he need not be unmarried, and, indeed, that he need not be a "he" at all?

Every Catholic would readily admit that a bishop need not wear a jewelled ring nor be addressed as "Your Excellency." But do we also realize that the

22

bishop need not have the power to assign and change priests; that he need not have any financial or administrative responsibilities at all; that he need not wear clerical clothing; that he need not be unmarried, and, like the pope, that he need not be a "he" at all?

Every Catholic would readily admit that the sacraments need not be celebrated in a special language (such as Latin). But do we also realize that a sacrament need not be celebrated in exactly the same manner each time; that the celebrant need not always wear the distinctively "religious" garments prescribed in the official liturgical books; that the roles of the various participants need not always be uniform and absolutely unchanging; that the form of some sacraments (e.g., private confession) could disappear entirely from the life and practice of the Church?

The point here is neither to espouse each of these possible changes nor to confuse and infuriate those Catholics who are most uneasy about changes in the Church. A theologian remains a servant of the Church. His task is the assistance of the faithful in coming to a better understanding of the Gospel as it has been proclaimed by the Lord himself in Sacred Scripture, by the early Church, and by the Church of his own day. But it is my firm conviction that the Catholic Church is in its present difficulties precisely because of the theological gap that has existed for too long between the professionals and the rest of the community, and sometimes between professional and professional (witness, for example, the remarkable gap between the theology that had been taught for the most part in the major pontifical universities in Rome and the theology that actually permeated most of the council documents).

Otherwise intelligent and well educated Catholics were totally unprepared for the Second Vatican Council and have been utterly frightened by the forces which that council released throughout the whole Christian world. They have been profoundly upset by discussions within the Church about the authority of the pope, the administration of the sacraments, the social and political implications of the Gospel, the role of priests and religious, variations in catechetical formation and theological expression, apparent changes in moral outlook, and so forth.

This is the time for plainer speaking, because language has a way of being conveniently misinterpreted. Even the racist applauds the rhetoric of patriotism with its ringing call for "liberty and justice for all;" the militarist nods his assent when sane men speak for peace; and who among us is not for "law and order?" The rhetoric of religious language can have an equally numbing effect on many of us, unless and until we occasionally hit upon an issue that intrudes upon the actual human experience of many people, such as the regulation of births.

24

If the Catholic Church is to exercise any kind of meaningful influence in the world for the sake of the Kingdom of God, it has to recognize that the mistakes of the past cannot be repeated. Catholics must be prepared for what is to come by being honestly confronted with what is and what has been.

4. The Question of Catholicity

Michael Novak's September, 1969, *Commonweal* article ("Where Did All the Spirit Go?") attracted some favorable comment in the Catholic press. A philosopher of liberal and reformist persuasion, Novak argues that too many of his colleagues in the struggle for change have become preoccupied with institutional and political tugging-and-pulling. It is a point that has since been made by Father Andrew Greeley in his weekly syndicated column.

It is assumed that the whole problem with the Church is structural and that, once the old walls have come down and a new scaffolding erected under more amiable auspices, nearly all the annoyances now besetting us will have disappeared.

What the liberal and radical Catholic today seems to lack, Novak suggests, is "a sense of participation in a life divine as well as human." They do not see that institutional reform is for the sake of a Christian life of higher quality and of deeper roots. The present structure of Roman Catholicism must be altered, but in a virtually total way.

That means that the reform must reach even into those areas where the secularist will not tread. Reform must be concerned as much with prayer and contemplation, with joy and thanksgiving, with celebration of God's presence in the world, as with collegiality and constitutionalism.

There is also some criticism of those at the opposite end of the Catholic spectrum, particularly those who reduce the whole crisis in the Church today to one of faith, or the lack thereof. Novak wonders what they have in mind with their appeal to faith.

"They seem to mean a resolve of will to think about things (or at least to speak about things) in a special way, in a special language, structuring all their perceptions accordingly," he writes. "Or else they seem to mean an undisturbed, unquestioned, simple way of life . . . "

Both are properly rejected. Faith is not ideology (i.e., a body of "truths" and principles whose primary function and intent is the preservation of the institution which issues them), nor is it blind and uncritical thinking.

Thus far, Novak's arguments are on the mark. He has managed to hit some slow moving targets on both left and right. The heart of the problem, however, is not what's wrong with certain liberals and conservatives, but what is the positive alternative to their attitudes and views? In other words, what does

it mean to be a Catholic? It is at this point that Novak's forward thrust begins to falter.

"I conclude that they are Catholic who think of
themselves as Catholic, and who shape their lives
(in quite personally and culturally distinct ways)
around reflection on the Word, the celebration of the
eucharist, and a universal sense of peoplehood."

If the word "eucharist" is taken in a wider sense
(embracing the Orthodox, Anglican, and Protestant
liturgies), then this definition of catholicity is too
broad. It could apply to any Christian. Nor is it
enough to say that one is a Catholic who thinks of
himself as a Catholic (no more than one could say
that he is open-minded and tolerant because he
thinks of himself as open-minded and tolerant).

Novak rejects a caricature of the idea that Catholicism is distinguished by its affirmation of papacy
and episcopacy within the context of collegiality:
"The centralized structure around Pope and Curia,
and the use of Rome as a symbol for universal peoplehood, now seem inadequately Catholic, neither true
enough nor human enough nor close enough to the
Gospels." But he seems to reject more than the
caricature.

The specific nature of Catholicism seems, in this
view, to be a matter of cultural rather than theological or doctrinal reality: "Catholic faith is more
adequately placed in a people, with all the faults—
personal, social, cultural, and institutional — of

27

peoples." Catholics are those who have been shaped by a special history and who could not erase that network of memories, sentiments, and images even if they tried. Presumably, therefore, Charles Davis is still a Catholic, even though he insists that he is not.

A more doctrinal and theological approach is provided in the second chapter of the Dogmatic Constitution on Divine Revelation. Catholicism is more than a cultural mentality; it is a matter of perceiving a special relationship among revelation, faith, Sacred Scripture, tradition, magisterium, and theology, and of structuring ecclesiastical life (however loosely) around this perception.

The entire second chapter of *Dei Verbum* is concerned with the relationships that exist among revelation, faith, Scripture, tradition, doctrine, and theology. In other words, this chapter raises the question: how does the individual Christian and the Church as a whole come to *understand* the Gospel of Jesus Christ, and by what process does the Christian reduce this understanding to *language,* whether written or spoken? There is no question more basic than this.

It is one thing for us to say that we believe that Jesus is the Lord, or that he has redeemed man from sin by his death and resurrection, or that the Church is the Body of Christ, or that the Christian is justified by faith and baptism, or that the Church is built on

28

the foundation of the Apostles (and the prophets) and today on the foundation of the college of bishops with the pope at its center and head, or that God will be faithful to his promises by bringing all creation under his reign at the end of history.

But it is quite another matter to be able to say *how* we have come to these expressions of belief and *on what basis* do we use such language to describe these central convictions about God, Christ, the Church, redemption, and human history.

How we perceive and express the Gospel of Jesus Christ is at the root of the differences between Catholics and other Christians. It is certainly not a question of greater spirituality or holiness on the part of the Catholic, nor of more profound theological insight, nor of a higher regard for the supernatural order, and so on. Nor is it only a matter, as some have suggested, of cultural differences based on varieties of historical experience.

As Hans Küng wrote on the eve of Vatican II in his *The Council, Reform, and Reunion,* the fundamental issue dividing Catholics from their brother Christians is that of ecclesiastical office. Christians of differing traditions can, and often do, agree among themselves on the essential meaning of the Church as People of God, or on the Lordship of Jesus, or on the importance of sacramental celebration. But the issue on which fundamental argument develops is the issue of ecclesiastical office, specifically the question

29

of the authority held and exercised by the college of bishops with the pope at its center and head.

And this is not merely a question of external organization. On the contrary, one's idea of ecclesiastical office will determine one's understanding of the process by which a Christian comes to know the meaning of the Gospel and then puts that understanding into words.

Most Christians agree that we come to an understanding of the Gospel in several different ways and through several different sources: the Bible itself, the interpretations of the great Fathers of the Church (e.g., Irenaeus and Augustine), the documents of the early councils (e.g., Nicea and Chalcedon), the writings of the classic theologians of the past (e.g., Thomas and Calvin), and even some of the data offered by various nontheological disciplines (e.g., sociology and psychology).

But Christians do not agree on the role and authority of the college of bishops, and, more specifically, on the meaning of the papal office. Non-Catholic Christians generally do not acknowledge that the colleges of bishops has an irreplaceable function in holding in balance the various factors which make it possible to understand and to express the Gospel; namely, Scripture, tradition, and contemporary Christian experience.

Unlike his brother Christians, the Catholic accords antecedent attention and respect to the stated positions, past and present, of the Church's college of bishops, whether expressed collectively or through its spokesman, the bishop of Rome. That is to say, when the Catholic is trying to make up his mind about some matter that touches upon his understanding of the Gospel or upon its exercise in the ethical order, he will always give serious weight to the guidelines proposed from this official, collegial source.

There may be occasions, as in the recent controversy over *Humanae Vitae*, where, after examination of the teaching proposed by official sources, the Catholic will disagree with, or even resist, these guidelines. But this is always the exception rather than the rule. When the Catholic finds that he is constantly at odds with the stated positions of the Church's college of bishops, past and present, then he must reassess his initial acceptance of and commitment to the Catholic tradition as such. In other words, he must begin to ask himself: Why am I a Catholic?

But how does a Christian come to understand and to express the Gospel? How does he know that his notion of the Gospel is correct, that it is faithful to the Gospel's original meaning and intent?

To repeat: Catholics and Protestants agree that our vision of the Gospel is derived from, and determined by, the testimony of Sacred Scripture, the writings of the great Fathers of the Church, the documents of the early ecumenical councils, and the insights of the major theologians of the past.

We do not always agree, however, on the normative value of the doctrines and dogmas which have been formulated and proposed by the Church's college of bishops, or by the chief member of that college, namely the pope.

Catholics attribute special importance to the role of the college of bishops, in a way which has no equivalent in the rest of the Body of Christ. Catholics insist that, in making up one's mind about a matter of Christian faith or action, each member must consult and take into serious account not only the evidence of Scripture or the teachings of the first five ecumenical councils or the major statements of faith produced in the 16th century, but also the explicit and official positions adopted by the Church's college of bishops, both present and past.

This view, while reassuring to some Catholics, may appear excessively conservative to others. And yet we are faced with the question: What is it that really distinguishes the Catholic from the non-Catholic Christian if it is not, as Hans Küng suggested, their respective interpretations of *ecclesiastical office?*

The point is developed in two of Gregory Baum's recent books. He argues that the Catholic Church alone offers the possibility of creating a doctrinal consensus on matters of faith and morals. It has an understanding of postbiblical tradition unlike that of any other Christian church. Because of its distinctive understanding, the Catholic Church is best able to preserve the delicate balance between the past and the present, between the classic expressions of faith and the application of the Gospel to modern times and conditions.

"The Catholic Church believes that the process of formulating doctrine, which the Spirit produced in the past, continues to go on in the present," he writes in *The Credibility of the Church Today* (p. 146). "The divine tradition alive in the Church today enabled the Catholic Church to reinterpret her doctrinal position at Vatican II and renders her capable of continuing this in the future." (See also his *Faith and Doctrine*, pp. 95-98.)

Father Baum tends to claim too much in his apologetical argument on behalf of the Catholic Church, but he is at least conducting the argument at the right place, i.e., in the area of doctrinal formulation. Charles Davis, for an entirely different reason, substantiates this view. In his *Question of Conscience*, he too identifies the collegial structure of the Church as the distinctively Catholic feature of the Body of Christ, and he rejects Catholicism precisely at this point. For him, the teaching authority and unifying function of the college of bishops, including the pope, have lost their claim to credibility.

It is not enough to say, therefore, that Catholics are different from other Christians because they celebrate all seven sacraments, or because they assign special importance to the Blessed Virgin, or because they expect of one another weekly attendance at the Eucharist, and so forth. On such matters as these, the Catholic is often indistinguishable from, let us say, the Orthodox or the Anglo-Catholic. And yet even these Christian churches do not fully accept the Catholic's particular understanding of collegiality and of papal primacy within the college of bishops.

Chapter II of the Dogmatic Constitution on Divine Revelation is a matter of some relevance because it raises precisely this question. On the one hand, the chapter goes beyond some of the earlier and more rigid notions of Tradition, which tended to view Tradition as something totally independent of, and almost superior to, the testimony of Sacred Scripture. Scripture and Tradition were generally regarded by Catholics as two separate sources of Revelation. Vatican II did not reaffirm this opinion. On the contrary, it left the question open. This was, in itself, a major ecumenical advance.

But the same chapter continues to insist on the distinctively Catholic idea that the college of bishops plays an indispensable role in our understanding and expression of the Gospel. The frequently inept exercise of this magisterial office in our day should not be allowed to obscure this fundamental principle.

DISCUSSION QUESTIONS

1. Do you still think of the Catholic Church as the "one, true Church of Christ?" If so, where does

that leave the other Christian churches? What value, if any, do they have in the plan of Christ to bring about his Father's Kingdom in the world? If you no longer regard the Catholic Church as the "one, true Church of Christ," why do you think it matters if we are Catholics or not? Or doesn't it really matter?

2. Do you agree that the Catholic Church has tended, over the last hundred years since the First Vatican Council, to exaggerate the place of the pope in the Church and to overemphasize the importance of authority? If not, why do you think there has been so much debate within the Catholic Church recently about the pope in particular and about ecclesiastical authority in general? If you do agree that there has been an exaggeration of authority in the Catholic Church, why do you think that so many Catholics—laity, religious, and clergy alike—accepted it so uncritically for so long?

3. Do you think that the ecumenical movement has had a bad effect on convert-making? Do you think that these two apostolates are irreconcilable? Do you think that the ultimate goal of all Catholic activity in relation to non-Catholic Christians must be to bring the non-Catholic into the Catholic Church? If you do not think so, does that mean that you don't really think it makes any difference where one locates himself

or herself within the Body of Christ? In other words, how important is it to be or to become or to remain a Catholic Christian?

4. What do you understand by the biblical expression, "the Kingdom of God?" Do you tend to identify it with the Church? Do you separate the two realities completely? What relationship, if any, does the Church have with the Kingdom of God? Do you think our ideas about the Kingdom of God make any real difference with regard to our understanding of the nature and mission of the Church? If not, why not? If so, why?

5. It is often said that the Catholic Church has changed only in terms of accidentals. Do you think this is true, or do you suspect that there have been changes even in those doctrines or practices that you once thought could never change?

6. Have you ever used the term "collegiality" in conversation or in argument? What do you mean by it? Do you think our understanding of collegiality affects our understanding of the nature and mission of the Church? If not, why not? If so, why?

2

Faith and Dogma

1. The Crisis of Faith

There are at least three sides to the crisis of faith in the Catholic Church today: some Catholics don't believe enough, some Catholics believe too much, and some Catholics don't care either way.

They don't believe enough who reduce the meaning of "God" to the experience of fellowship and community, to the passion for social justice and peace, to a sense of personal commitment, or to various manifestations of love and friendship.

But they believe too much about God who look upon him as a kind of Superbeing manipulating man in a supremely arbitrary and self-serving fashion, who waters arid fields only after hearing a novena of prayers for rain, who bathes a picnic area with sunshine at the sight of rosary beads hung outside a window, or who punishes a young married couple by inflicting some severe physical deformity upon their newly-born child.

Catholics believe too little about Jesus of Nazareth when they regard him simply as one of several great historical figures, an example and a pattern for us all, a man whose ethical teaching and posture we applaud and strive to emulate, but one not significantly different from any other man except in the

37

degree to which he reveals the mystery and meaning of life to each one of us.

But they believe too much about Jesus who think of him in divine categories only, as God dressed up as man, as one who, from the moment of his birth (if not from the moment of his conception), knew all things and was in complete and perfect control of himself and of his environment. And these Catholics look upon his life and ministry as if their all-consuming purpose were the establishment of the Roman Catholic Church and the conferral of the keys of the Kingdom upon St. Peter.

Catholics believe too little about the Church when they regard it as so thoroughly human an organization that it can be changed or eliminated at will, without concern for its origins or its history. The Church, in this view, is nothing more or less than the sum total of people who share a common attitude toward God and Jesus. It operates under the usual laws of sociology and psychology and can be manipulated accordingly. Its various structural elements (e.g., the Petrine office, the college of bishops, or the sacraments) are eminently dispensable.

But they believe too much about the Church who identify it with the Kingdom of God, who assume that the Church is where God is most actively and and most fruitfully engaged in the processes of history, who think that membership in the Church somehow assures one of ultimate personal salvation or at least gives him a running headstart over the rest of men.

Catholics believe too little about the Eucharist when they judge it to be not essentially different from any common meal. Every Eucharist is a fellowship experience, and every fellowship experience is a Eucharist. Whether there is any explicit memorial or celebration of the redemptive deeds of Jesus is really beside the point.

But they believe too much about the Eucharist who think it to be the only place where the Lord is really and truly present and accessible to his people, who regard the Mass as a new immolation of Jesus and a new act of atonement, as if his "once-for-all" sacrifice were not sufficient, and who assume that Communion is somewhat a reward for virtue and, as such, something to be received on the rarest of occasions.

Catholics believe too little about the Petrine office when they think of it not only as a dispensable ingredient in the Body of Christ but as something positively obstructive of the Kingdom of God. They believe too little about the pope when they make of him simply a bishop among bishops, whose witness and whose mission is no different from that of any other ecclesiastical functionary.

But they believe too much about the papacy who think of its occupant as a kind of absolute monarch, a law unto himself, who can, by the will of Christ, do anything he chooses, in whatever way he chooses. The bishops are merely his delegates, and every Catholic his faithful subject. The pope is closest to God and therefore closest to God's truth. The good Catholic will never think or act differently from the pope's expressed wishes and views.

However wide of the mark these two groups appear to be, they continue to take seriously, in their own distinctive ways, the traditional symbols of faith (God, Christ, Church, etc.). But there are many Catholics for whom these symbols have no meaning or interest at all. These people may constitute the greatest problem of all for the Church. The crisis of faith could be deepest here.

2. Questions and Doubts

Many Catholics believe that because everything seems to be in question today, everything is also in doubt. This is not true.

First, although Christian theologians can never tire of asking the question, "Who is God?", they do not doubt that there is more to life than meets the eye, that there is a ground of being, a beyond in our midst, a gracious reality which gives direction, purpose, and meaning to human life and history.

These theologians may question the validity of speaking of God in scholastic or Aristotelian categories alone. They may experiment with process philosophy, or existentialism, or depth psychology in

40

order to provide a better understanding of the divine reality. But such probing does not put the divine reality itself in fundamental doubt.

If a person does not believe in the reality of God in any sense, he is neither Christian nor religious. That does not mean necessarily that he lacks faith totally and, therefore, cannot hope for salvation. Men can have implicit faith, and by this implicit faith they can be saved. But to be religious and, all the more, to be Christian requires some explicit acknowledgement of the reality and sovereignty of God.

Secondly, although Christian theologians raise serious questions about Jesus of Nazareth (they ask, for example, about the growth of his self-consciousness: when and how did he become aware of his messianic role?), they do not doubt his uniqueness or his ultimacy in human history. Jesus is the Christ, and there is no other.

It is true, of course, that some theologians of Christian and Catholic background have questioned this identification of Jesus of Nazareth with the Christ of faith. (I am not referring here to Bultmann). I do not challenge the sincerity or the seriousness with which these views are put forth. I do challenge the assumption that such views are compatible with Christian faith.

It is a fact beyond dispute, it seems to me, that Christian faith is distinguished and set apart from every other kind of religious faith or intellectual perspective by its affirmation of the Lordship of Jesus of Nazareth. Jesus is not only a principal manifestation of the Christ of faith; he *is* the Christ of faith.

One may decide, after nineteen centuries, that Jesus of Nazareth is not, in fact, the Lord of history, that the traditional Christian confessions about him were wrong. But that decision, however carefully formulated it may be, places one outside the circle of Christian faith. If Jesus is not the Lord, there is no basis at all for Christian faith.

Thirdly, although many theologians today are raising important questions about the Church (they ask about the scope of its mission and about some of its historical forms, e.g., the monarchical episcopate, a canonically supreme papacy, etc.), they do not fundamentally doubt that the Church is a mystery of faith, that it somehow embodies the presence of Christ in history in a way that has no exact reduplication anywhere else, in such wise that the Church can be described, in the Pauline sense, as the very Body of Christ.

The Church is not a casual organization of people who happen to share similar views of life and history. It is an assembly *called forth by God* (which is the meaning of the Greek word from which we derive our word, "church"). Its membership is determined not only by personal choice, but by the election of God. Indeed, the latter element is the decisive one.

42

(I am not suggesting here that every member of the Church can be certain that he belongs in the Church by divine election. The perception of God's call is always a matter of prudential judgment on our part, and, therefore, always subject to error.)

Fourthly, Catholic theologians have raised new questions about the Real Presence of Christ in the Eucharist. They have proposed that the scholastic, Aristotelian notion of transubstantiation may not, in fact, be the best explanation of the Eucharistic mystery for our time, and they have offered in its place other explanations based on different philosophical world-views.

These theologians have not challenged the historic Catholic faith (shared by other Christians, too) that Christ is really and truly present in the bread and wine in a way not reduplicated anywhere else. We properly reverence those consecrated elements and we believe that our reception of them brings us into a new and unique sacramental relationship with Christ and with one another.

Everything may seem to be in question today, but not everything is in doubt. I do not suggest, however, that nothing is in doubt. There are many items of Christian belief and practice which are not matters of faith but rather matters of cultural, political, and historical development. These items are open not only to question but even, if one has good reasons, to doubt.

3. *Some Areas of Doubt*

Everyone who doubts, questions. But not everyone who questions, doubts. A doubt is a question which carries with it an inclination not to believe. It is a question tinged with scepticism.

In the previous section I used this distinction with reference to matters of Christian faith. I think that many Catholics mistakenly believe that that because everything seems to be in question today, everything is also in doubt.

There are no areas of theology which are beyond the range of questioning, but there *are* areas which are beyond the range of doubt. Thus, a theologian (or any Christian) may raise fundamental questions about God, Christ, and the Church, but he does not cross the line between questioning and doubting until he begins to suspect that God is unreal, that Jesus is nothing more than a first-century apocalyptic figure, or that the Church is an organization exactly like any other human organization, without any special grounding in the call of God the Father or the unifying presence of his Spirit.

Each of these realities—God, Christ, and Church —has, in fact, been the subject of doubt, even by some theologians and writers with a Christian and Catholic background. I said previously that, in my judgment, none of these realities can be the subject of radical doubt without, at the same time, moving the doubter outside the circle of Christian faith.

I did not say, however, that doubt is totally incompatible with Christian faith. There are many items associated with Christian belief and practice which, in my opinion and in the judgment of others, have begun to lose much of their earlier credibility.

In other words, it is entirely possible that a Catholic could, in good conscience, say that he really doesn't see the point of this or that belief and practice.

There are some examples which are so obvious that they are no longer even controversial. Thus, a Catholic who doubted (i.e., questioned with a sense of scepticism) the suitability of celebrating Mass with the priest facing the back wall of the church was on good theological grounds and, indeed, history has vindicated his doubt.

The same line of reasoning would apply to his attitude toward Latin in the Mass, the participation of the laity in the mission of the Church, the change of the laws of fast and abstinence, the celebration of Mass at a mixed marriage, intercommunion (under limited circumstances), collegiality, and so forth.

At various times in the recent history of the Church, those who supported reforms in each of these areas have incurred the suspicion (if not the wrath) of many fellow Catholics. The resistance to the liturgical movement in the thirties, forties, and even into the fifties, is very well known. Today, one cannot be anti-liturgical without, at the same time, being unfaithful to the Second Vatican Council and, therefore, to the legitimate authority of the Church.

There are other items, however, which are of a more controversial nature. I am listing some of them here. Undoubtedly there will be some Catholics who will believe that these items are not, in fact, subject to doubt (at most, one may raise questions about them, but even that exercise is a little risky). They will assume that raising doubts about such items is tantamount to denying Christian faith. Obviously, I do not agree.

(1) A Catholic may doubt that Jesus of Nazareth, from the moment of his birth, knew everything there was to know about life, about history, about science, or even about his own messianic mission.

(2) A Catholic may doubt that divine providence means that God actually sends sickness to people, causes accidents, makes people lose (or gain) jobs, or, in general, actively manipulates every human and historical event, and is himself manipulatable by prayers of petition.

(3) A Catholic may doubt the traditional explanation of original sin; namely, that each one of us is now subject to sin, sickness, and death because of something two particular people did many centuries ago in the Garden of Paradise.

(4) A Catholic may doubt a non-infallible teaching of the pope.

(5) A Catholic may doubt the traditional assumption that only Roman Catholic priests (and perhaps Orthodox priests, too) are validly ordained, and, therefore, only Catholic Masses (with the same qualification regarding the Orthodox) are true expressions of the Eucharist to any extent or degree.

The reader should notice that I did not say that a Catholic *should* doubt these items, nor have I suggested that there is something naive about the faith of a Catholic who does not, in fact, doubt these items.

My concern in this section is as much pastoral as theological. Many Catholics are troubled by questions and doubts about the faith. It is important that we see the difference between a question and a doubt, and also that we have some idea of the legitimacy and extent of raising doubts as well as straightforward, but trusting, questions.

4. Does Doctrine Change?

Every Catholic over 25 or 30 must be struck by the extent and intensity of change that the Church has experienced in the last 10 years.

There have been changes in the way we celebrate the central act of worship, the Mass; changes in our sacramental habits and practice; changes in our attitude toward sin and virtue; changes in the lifestyle of priests and religious; changes in the use and exercise of ecclesiastical authority; changes in the way Catholics respond to the directives of such authority; changes in many of the laws and customs of the Church; changes in the relations between Catholics and non-Catholic Christians, especially in matters of common worship and marriage; and so forth.

The Second Vatican Council and Pope John XXIII account, in such large measure, for many of these changes in Catholic attitudes and practice. But some would argue that these changes would have happened eventually anyway. They would point to the introductory section of *Gaudium et Spes* (the Pastoral Constitution on the Church in the Modern World) for support.

The "signs of the times" were emerging independently of religion in general and of the Church in particular: the breakdown of traditional social customs and institutions, the growth of city living, the explosion in the communications industry, the remarkable increase in human mobility, enormous technological progress on several fronts, and the quest for political liberation and self-determination by the smaller nations and by minority groups within the larger ones (see arts. 4-10, especially art. 6).

At the beginning of the last decade, most Catholics would have questioned practically nothing; by the end of the decade, many Catholics were questioning everything. So much had changed; why not doctrines too? Must we continue to believe in original sin? What makes the Church any different from any other service-oriented organization? Why should we accord any special importance to the pope and the bishops? Should ordination be necessary for the exercise of the ministry of preaching and worship? Is Christ really present in the Eucharist? Is Jesus really the Lord?

A firm, hardline approach seems to have developed among some other Catholics in reaction against this new questioning spirit. There is a heart and center to the Christian faith, they argue, which is not subject to change in any sense—that which was believed from the very beginning by everyone, everywhere. "Development" is distortion.

This was, in fact, the general view which permeated the documents of Trent and Vatican I. "Any meaning of the sacred dogmas that has once been declared by holy mother Church must always be retained," the First Vatican Council stated in its important Constitution on Faith, "and there must never be any deviation from that meaning on the specious grounds of a more profound understanding."

The Second Vatican Council, however, endorses neither position. It does not suggest, as some Catholics now argue, that every major tenet of Christian faith has been submerged in a sea of radical doubt. Nor does the council propose that doctrines are so immutable that they are not subject to development of any kind.

There is, on the one hand, a tradition which comes from the Apostles and which is developed within the

Church by the assistance of the Holy Spirit. But there is also a genuine "growth in the understanding of the realities and the words which have been handed down" (Dogmatic Constitution on Divine Revelation, art. 8, para. 2).

"For as the centuries succeed one another," the council states, "the Church constantly moves forward toward the fullness of divine truth until the words of God reach their complete fulfillment in her."

Every generation in the Church struggles to understand the Gospel in a way that really makes sense in terms of its own peculiar experience. We cannot simply and uncritically appropriate the language and concepts of previous times, even of the primitive community of the New Testament.

We are assured of a basic continuity between our contemporary understanding and that of previous generations not only by the presence of the Holy Spirit but also by the existence of a legitimate teaching authority centered in, although not exclusively limited to, the college of bishops.

It is true that this latter affirmation is questioned more and more by Catholics themselves. Without it, however, the distinctively Catholic understanding of the Body of Christ evaporates.

5. Faith and Dogma

The development of dogma is one of the most difficult problems in all of theology. I have the impression, however, that many Catholics regard this question as open-and-shut. If the Church officially taught anything in the past, the teaching must still be true today, even though, for the sake of modernity, a few words and expressions may have been changed here and there along the line.

A faithful Catholic, according to this point of view, is one who accepts the teaching of the Church as it stands. He is a fundamentally secure person because he knows that history cannot corrode the truth of this teaching. It was sound doctrine when it was first presented with full ecclesiastical authority, and it remains sound and authoritative doctrine today.

What about those Christians who do not accept all the doctrines of the Catholic Church? How can we enter into sincere dialogue with them if we believe from the start that they refuse to live by *all* the teachings of Christ?

These same Catholics would say that we should be pleasant and understanding toward the non-Catholic Christian but, in the final accounting, the non-Catholic must come our way, not vice versa. Eventually, he simply must acknowledge the truth of every single Catholic doctrine, as proposed by the councils of the Church and in the official declarations of the popes.

Thus, for all practical purposes, every Protestant would have to accept the doctrine of the Real Presence of Christ in the Eucharist in precisely the same way as it was taught to Catholics in the Baltimore Catechism, i.e., according to the specific understanding of transubstantiation common among Catholic theologians at the time.

And every Protestant, Anglican, and Orthodox Christian alike would have to accept the pope as the absolute ruler of the Church according to the same idea of the Church that prevailed among theologians of the late 19th and early 20th centuries.

The same would be true of the teachings on original sin, atonement, Mariology, the institution of the seven sacraments by Christ, and so forth.

If this line of reasoning is correct, then indeed there is no real problem at all regarding "dogmatic development." Once the Church issues an official formulation of faith, it is final and absolute. The kernel of truth cannot change; only the husk of language changes. Dogma, in other words, is on a par with the Word of God itself. It embodies revelation in a way that is different from Sacred Scripture, but it is no less authoritative and binding.

This was the usual Catholic understanding of "dogmatic development" as recently as the early 1960's, and many, as I have suggested, still hold to it. When the late Cardinal Bea spoke at the Roman-Catholic-Protestant Colloquium held at Harvard

University several years ago, he felt bound by the canons of ecumenical honesty to remind his non-Catholic listeners that the Catholic Church would not—because it could not—change the dogmas already "on the books."

He implied, in fact, that the dogmas of the Church were on a par with the Word of God itself: "The Church has solemnly proclaimed all these doctrines to be of faith, that is to say, truths revealed by God himself and necessary for salvation."

The Church's responsibility toward these truths of faith is to guard, explain, and defend them, but never to compromise them. "For the Church founded by Christ cannot tamper with the Word of God which he preached and entrusted to her care" (see *Dialogue at Harvard,* edited by S. Miller and G. Wright, Harvard University Press, 1964, pp. 63-4).

The Second Vatican Council has moved somewhat beyond this particular notion of the immutability of dogma: "There is a growth in the understanding of the realities and the words which have been handed down . . . For as the centuries succeed one another, the Church constantly moves forward toward the fullness of divine truth until the words of God reach their fulfillment in her" *(Dei Verbum,* art. 8).

Is it possible any longer to imply that dogma is on a par with revelation itself? Can we continue to assume that each dogma contains an objective kernel

53

of truth which cannot be affected by the passage of time and the development of history?

Dare we suggest that dogmas can change—not just the words, but even the meaning? And are dogmas such that, once proclaimed, they must be believed by every Christian according to a single intended meaning?

For some of the following material, I am indebted to a very constructive article by Father Avery Dulles, S.J., "Dogma as an Ecumenical Problem," which first appeared in *Theological Studies* (September, 1968). The essay was reprinted in *Catholic Mind* (May, 1969), a popular, nonacademic magazine. This indicates how successful Father Dulles was in confronting a timely, but scholarly, topic with exceptional clarity and force.

I can do no more than summarize his arguments and conclusions, with the hope that some interested readers will actually seek out the full text.

The concept of dogma as a fixed formula of faith— i.e., containing an unchangeable kernel of truth which must be believed by all, for all time—is of relatively recent vintage. It is not in the Bible, the writings of the Fathers, nor even in medieval Scholasticism.

Rather, the concept seems to have its origin in a book written in 1792 by a Franciscan, Philipp Neri Chrismann, wherein he states that "a dogma of the faith is nothing other than a divinely revealed doctrine and truth, which is proposed by the public judgment of the Church as something to be believed by divine faith, in such wise that the contrary is condemned by the Church as heretical doctrine."

Many Catholics, including even those who have undertaken formal studies in theology, would probably have no difficulty at all with this definition.

But what is remarkable about it is that the definition was assailed by many theologians at the time because it seemed too narrow and minimalistic in its understanding of dogma, and Chrismann's work was placed on the Index of Forbidden Books.

His idea, however, was only repressed, not destroyed. In the 19th century, when Christian faith came under the attack of the new rationalism, Chrismann's authoritarian view of dogma was taken up by Catholic apologists as a very convenient weapon.

Catholics do not have to worry about the intellectual basis of their faith. They need not get involved in fruitless and confusing arguments. The teaching authority of the Church is the supreme guide that can lead wayward Catholics out of the morass of rationalistic speculation and into the clear, crisp air of dogmatic certainty and security.

Chrismann's notion of dogma reappeared in the official Roman documents of the period: the Syllabus of Errors (1864), the constitutions of Vatican I (1869-70), and the anti-Modernist documents (1907-10).

"To ward off naturalistic rationalism," Dulles observes, "orthodox theology adopted a supernaturalistic rationalism in which revelation was conceived as a divinely imparted system of universal and timeless truths entrusted to the Church as teacher."

Vatican II advanced considerably beyond this view. In its Dogmatic Constitution on Divine Revelation, the council depicts revelation as happening in and through the events of history, and particularly in and through the central Christ-event. The principal purpose of revelation is not so much the communication of information about God as it is an occasion of interpersonal communication between God and man. (The theological argument for this latter judgment is contained in an article by Gregory Baum, "Vatican II's Constitution on Revelation," *Theological Studies*, March, 1967.)

The expanded understanding of revelation which is reflected in the council document has prompted a reconsideration of the meaning of dogma. Postconciliar Catholic theology is now calling into question at least four important features of the Neo-Scholastic notion of dogma: its identity with revelation, its conceptual objectivity (kernel of truth), its immutability (an *unchanging* kernel of truth), and its universality (dogmas are to be accepted by all Christians; the unity of the Church is impossible without such prior dogmatic agreement).

56

The words are long, and they have a certain technical ring to them. But many will recognize here an issue of major practical and pastoral importance. Much of the frustration, distress, and anguish present in the Catholic Church today arises, in large part, from a basic confusion about this relationship between faith and dogma.

The reader should not forget the opening sentence of this section: "The development of dogma is one of the most difficult problems in all of theology." As good as it is, Father Dulles' article, "Dogma as an Ecumenical Problem," does not eliminate all the complexities of the question. And neither can my summary of his views hope to do that.

What I am urging here is not that Catholics should suddenly adopt an indifferent, laissez-faire attitude toward the doctrines of the Church. One formulation of the Christian faith is not necessarily equal to another. On the contrary, some explanations of Christian faith are distorted and, therefore, unacceptable. The role of the college of bishops within the Church is to help the Christian community sort out what is viable and correct from what is weak and misleading.

The formulation of dogma is one way—although certainly not the only way—in which the college of bishops exercises its service to the Church. There are times, in other words, when a major issue of faith is at stake and where conflicting and competing views of that faith have created a situation of wide-spread and dangerous confusion. The history of the ecumenical councils provides a record of such official interventions into controversies about the Gospel.

Our first question: Are these dogmatic formulae on par with revelation itself? The answer is "No," or at least "Not necessarily." Revelation, first of all, cannot be limited to spoken or written words, nor do such words of themselves constitute revelation. *Dei Verbum* widens the notion of revelation to encompass both word and *event*.

"In the formulas of faith," Father Dulles notes, "we catch fleeting glimpses of the divine truth toward which our whole being is tending. The truth of the revealing God cannot be reduced to the dead letter of any doctrinal affirmation, yet such an affirmation may become God's revelatory word. Because revelation is eschatological, dogma always points to a future disclosure beyond all history."

The second question: Is there a kernel of objective truth resting beneath the husk of language in a dogmatic formulation? Protestant and Anglican theologians (e.g., Schlink and I. T. Ramsey) are not alone in criticizing a literalistic or fundamentalistic notion of dogma. Karl Rahner, S.J., has made a similar criticism ("What is a Dogmatic Statement?" in *Theological Investigations*, vol. V, pp.58-60). One cannot say that a dogmatic formula is so descriptive of a particular reality that it can be tested for accuracy by scientific means.

Even the conservative Catholic theologian, Hans Urs von Balthasar, concurs in this general view: "(Dogmas) are true insofar as they are a function and expression of the Church's understanding of the Christ-mystery, as given to it by the Holy Spirit. They cannot be taken out of this setting; therefore, they do not have any *purely* theoretical (i.e., non-experiential, non-existential) truth" (*Concilium,* vol. 21, p. 90).

A third question: Once a dogmatic statement is hammered out, must it remain unchanged forever? Can more than the words be altered? Dulles reminds us that surprising changes in the verbal tests of orthodoxy have occurred in the course of Church history. Not only have there been differences of wording, but even differences of concepts. Indeed, one cannot easily separate concepts from language. To speak of language simply as the husk of an unchangeable truth misunderstands both language and truth. The transformation of the axiom, "Outside the Church no salvation," is a case in point.

This formula was proposed in the most stringent terms by popes and councils in the Middle Ages (e.g., Boniface VIII, Lateran Council IV, and the Council of Florence). It was understood (and intended to be understood) in this literal sense: those outside the Catholic Church cannot be saved.

Catholic theologians today usually suggest that the formula not be employed at all any longer, especially in preaching. It is almost always subject to misunderstanding. Furthermore, it conflicts in spirit, if not in fact, with the Second Vatican Council's emphasis on the availability of salvation outside the Church (e.g., *Lumen Gentium,* art. 16). It seems clear enough that the original understanding of the formula is no longer accepted. And we haven't even changed the words.

Most Catholics, including many theologians, have generally taken it for granted that a dogma, once it has been proposed for belief by the Magisterium, ought to be accepted by everyone throughout the Church.

Father Dulles recalls that such was not even the case in the New Testament where we have a variety of creedal affirmations traceable to various segments of the primitive Church.

And later on, various local churches were content to have their own particular creeds. Until the conversion of Constantine, when the Church became the official religion of the Roman Empire, the recitation of identical creeds was not considered essential to Christian unity.

The Council of Florence, in the 15th century, affirmed that the unity of the Church should be built not on particular doctrinal formulations but rather "on the cornerstone, Christ Jesus, who will make both one."

Accordingly, the Latins were permitted to retain the use of the *Filioque* in their Creed (i.e., they continued to profess that the Holy Spirit proceeds from the Father *and the Son*), while the Greeks could omit the *Filioque* and subscribe to the formula "from the Father *through* the Son."

The decision amounted to a recognition that the revealed truth about the inner life of the Trinity was so rich that it could not be captured by either of the two formulas. They were seen instead as expressing different aspects of the same mystery.

"Thus the Council of Florence," Father Dulles concludes, "implicitly rejected the equation 'one faith—one dogma.' It acknowledged that there can be a dogmatic statement which is, from a certain point of view, valid and orthodox, but which need not be imposed on believers who look at it from another angle."

This valid principle of dogmatic pluralism was obscured during the Counter-Reformation period, and to an even greater extent in the 19th century when the Church confronted the challenge of rationalism and relativism.

Pluralism reasserted itself, however, at the Second Vatican Council in its Decree on Ecumenism (articles 17 and 18), and the Dogmatic Constitution on the Church (art. 13) where it is stated that the local churches may retain their own distinctive traditions without prejudice to the overall unity of the Church.

These recent theological views on faith and dogma (and they are not peculiar to Father Dulles, as his footnote references would indicate) have significant ecumenical implications.

Ecumenical dialogue, after all, is fruitful only when it serves the double function of making us critical of our own formulations of faith and of awakening us to the authentic values in other traditions.

The current ecumenical dialogue imposes on all parties the obligation to reexamine their own formulations of faith to see what they have really meant all along. Sometimes we may find good theological reasons for the rejection of our views. In those cases, we must be prepared to revise and reformulate our earlier affirmations.

Secondly, each community within the Body of Christ must be ready to see a given dogmatic formulation from the other Church's point of view. We are finding already that some major dogmatic statements admit of other, more ecumenical, interpretations.

Thus, there is a sense in which a Catholic can accept the notions of *sola fide, sola gratia, soli Deo gloria,* etc. And there should be a sense in which Protestants can accept, for example, the sacramental principle long espoused and defended by the Catholic Church, or even the Catholic understanding of collegiality and the papal office.

Protestants have usually spoken of the Church as "at once holy and sinful" (*simul justus et peccator*), and therefore as something always to be reformed (*semper reformanda*). Vatican II's *Lumen Gentium* speaks of the Church as being "at the same time holy and always in need of being purified" (art. 8).

This is no mere coincidence. We seem to be recognizing more and more today that there is a wider basis for theological and even dogmatic agreement than we previously supposed.

We have not solved the problem of the relationship between faith and dogma. These remarks are still in the category of theological reflection, not certain and unassailable truth. But they open up avenues of possibilities which we cannot afford to ignore.

6. *The Limits of Orthodoxy*

In the preceding pages I have been raising the question of the relationship between faith and dogma. The problem is not an easy one to discuss, particularly when one's readership is general rather than specialized. It is not always possible to anticipate areas of misunderstanding or to avoid completely the impression of indifference to doctrinal truth or to episcopal and papal authority.

To sidestep the question entirely, however, does serve any real pastoral purpose. On the contrary, the frustration and distress that are evident in various sectors of the Catholic Church today reflect, in such large measure, a fundamental confusion regarding this matter of faith-and-dogma.

Many Catholics are saying: "If the Church taught us something in the past and now it wants to change its mind, why should we believe what the Church is teaching us now? If the Church could have been in error before, why can't it be in error today?" To raise the question of faith-and-dogma, therefore, is to open a Pandora's box.

For this reason many Catholics would prefer to be left with the uncomplicated idea that the teaching authority of the Church will tell them what to believe and what not to believe. And, no doubt, some are happy with this arrangement. My purpose in these essays is neither to ridicule their position nor to dislodge their opinions by force and violence.

My immediate concern, however, is for the many other Catholics who are troubled by this traditional explanation, and who find it very difficult to adjust to the changes in the world on the basis of that explanation alone. They are wondering if being a good, "orthodox" Catholic means simply accepting all the teachings "on the books," exactly as they have been explained to them at home, in catechism class, in parochial school, from the pulpit, and perhaps even in college or seminary.

The question that some Catholic theologians are raising today is whether orthodoxy is insured by the mere repetition of this cluster of teachings. Is a Catholic "orthodox" just because he can recite the words of a particular ecumenical council or papal document, and *says* that he believes in the words one hundred percent?

Several years ago Father Karl Rahner, S.J., suggested that heresy still exists in the Church, but it is no longer public. This charge would apply, it must be added, across the ecclesiastical spectrum—from Left to Right. The assumption that only the so-called liberal or progressive element in the Catholic Church has trouble with orthodoxy is unfair to that group and also naively ignores the equally persistent dangers of doctrinal error on the opposite side.

Father Dulles' comment is appropriate here: "Many . . . recite the orthodox formulas with so little understanding that their thoughts may well be heretical . . . the more one studies language, the more obvious it becomes that words are a poor test of right thinking. What most people call 'orthodoxy' really ought to be called 'orthophony'; it has to do with right speech rather than with right ideas."

Thus, it is possible that some Catholics, when pressed for a deeper explanation of their faith in the Trinity or the divinity of Christ, would reveal the notion that there are, for all practical purposes, three Gods (Tritheism), and that Jesus of Nazareth is not fully human, but that he is really God in the guise of man (Docetism).

The theologian (or the pope, the bishop, the priest, the religious, the teacher, *et al.*) does his fellow Catholics no service when he simply repeats and paraphrases earlier teachings and lets it go at that. Each doctrine, each text of Scripture, each liturgical and creedal formula, must *mean* something to the Church *here and now*. Mere verbal repetition does not, of itself, guarantee understanding or faith.

DISCUSSION QUESTIONS

1. Do you agree with the description of the crisis of faith in the first few pages of this chapter? If not, why not? If so, why? Do you think that oftentimes the "crisis of faith" is put in terms of too *little* faith rather than too *much* faith, which really means "credulity"? How do you understand the term "faith"? When you say something like, "That person has great faith," what do you mean?

2. Do you agree that, by and large, Catholic theologians are constructive in their intentions and in their work? If not, why not? What disturbs you most about the writings and statements of Catholic theologians? What is a "theologian"? Name five or six living Catholic theologians.

3. Could you add some other items to my list of doubts that Catholics today may legitimately entertain? Do you think that some of the items

I've placed on that list should not be there? Why not?

4. If you discovered that a doctrine once taught by an ecumenical council or a pope is no longer believable, would that induce you to leave the Catholic Church? If so, why? If not, why not? If your answer is "Yes," would you consider entering one of the other Christian churches? If so, why? If your answer is "No," what would you do? Would you become an agnostic, or join one of the non-Christian religions?

5. Do you think that doctrines serve any useful purpose at all? If so, what is that purpose? If not, why not?

6. Do you think that the sense of distress exhibited by some Catholics today in the face of doctrinal development, or even apparent change, is the result of theological factors only, or do you think that psychological factors are also involved? If so, which factors do you have in mind? If not, does that mean that you don't see any connection between the laws of human psychology and religious faith?

3

Theology and Dogma

1. The Theologian in the Church

What is the place and function of the theologian in the Church? An answer does not come easily.

Some Catholics tend to confuse the theologian's role with the episcopal and papal *magisterium*. Father Karl Rahner, for example, is pope; the international community of theologians (particularly those in Western Europe and the United States) is the college of bishops; major books and articles are the conciliar documents and encyclical letters; and press interviews and the more popular articles comprise the *ordinary magisterium*.

These Catholics seem to suggest that we can have a Church without pope and bishops, but we can't have a Church without theologians. And the term "theologian" includes anyone who lectures or writes on religious topics, even if his academic credentials are in some other area: philosophy, sociology, psychology, history, canon law, the classics, etc.

At the other extreme we have Catholics who regard all "theologians" as a danger to the Church (and they define the term about as broadly as I have in the previous paragraph). If it weren't for the so-called intellectuals probing around at the foundation of our historic faith, they argue, there wouldn't be so much confusion, controversy, and chaos in the Church today. Catholics would not be doubting the beliefs of their fathers; priests and nuns would not be questioning the structure and the value of their lives; and the authority of the Vicar of Christ on earth would be gratefully acknowledged rather than cynically ignored.

Theology is a difficult and a delicate enterprise. Its work is not aided or clarified by these kinds of friends and foes.

Christian theology is the systematic attempt to understand the meaning of the Gospel of Jesus Christ (as it is embodied in the Bible and in the history and present experience of the Church), and then to express that understanding in clear and coherent language.

The theologian is a theoretician by nature and by vocation. That is his service to the Church: to provide the theoretical principles by which the Church can justify (or criticize) what it *is* doing, or what it is *not* doing.

It should be obvious that the theologian and the Church official must work together. The theologian helps the pastoral leader to clarify, to sharpen, or even to modify his teaching and his preaching. The pastoral leader, on the other hand, provides the real-life questions without which theology becomes an abstract, academically sterile enterprise.

The pastoral leadership (and now I am speaking

particularly of the whole college of bishops, including therefore the pope as its center and head) has its own special charism to discern the Spirit in the midst of conflicting interpretations.

On occasion—and these are rare, as history testifies—the episcopal college will find that it must either endorse or reject a given position for the sake of the unity and integrity of the Church's life and mission. These official interventions (e.g., through a doctrinal formulation given at an ecumenical council) are, in turn, received by the theologian as new data upon which to reflect. They become new factors in the universal quest of theological understanding and expression.

There must also be tension, as well as cooperation, between the theological community and the leadership of the Church. The instincts of the latter will usually be conservative, i.e., they seek to protect the unity of the Church by providing the widest possible basis for agreement. Only rarely will the official magisterium so sharply define an issue that the definition actually drives some people out of the Church. The more frequent course will be to repeat the old formulas, already agreed upon and long since committed to "the books," rather than to risk confusion by new and different formulations.

The theologian, on the other hand, will want to press ahead, to question previous pronouncements, to ask if the "usual" mode of expression is best suited

71

for contemporary needs, to raise new questions not foreseen by councils and popes, past and present.

It is little wonder, therefore, that the work of the theologian (even the theologian with serious academic credentials and solid international reputation) is oftentimes regarded as a threat rather than an asset to the Church.

The phrase, "Don't rock the boat," reflects a basic truth about the human spirit. It does not readily embrace change, or the possibility of change. It seeks a resting place. Stability and sameness become signs of truth.

The theologian's job is to challenge that easy assumption. He does not thereby subvert the faith; he serves it—and he may even save it.

Indeed, faith cannot exist without theology. I do not mean that faith depends on theology in such wise that faith is *created* by theology. I am suggesting only that faith and theology are so interrelated that one cannot exist without the other. Let me illustrate the point.

I could suggest that each reader prepare a brief summary of his or her understanding of the Christian faith and then underline in red all those items in the summary which, in the reader's judgment, are absolutely essential for Christian orthodoxy (and, indeed, for Catholic orthodoxy). Most readers, I suppose, would not be at a loss for words, and the red pencil would probably get more than minimal use.

But then if I were to suggest a second project—namely, to provide answers to the questions, "What is theology?" and "How is theology related to revelation, faith, the Bible, tradition, and doctrine?" — I doubt if the pen would move with the same alacrity and grace.

Even in this period of questioning, doubt, and confusion, many Catholics still have some clear and basic personal convictions about God, Jesus Christ, redemption, the Church, the pope, original sin, and so forth. And yet, I would guess, a far smaller number has a sufficient grasp of the *process* by which we come to understand the Gospel and then express this understanding in words.

How we understand and articulate our common faith in Jesus Christ and in his Gospel is what Christian theology is all about. As soon as we try to explain our faith to other people (whether they are our children, our neighbors, our friends, our co-workers, our students, or even strangers), we are engaged in the work of theology. And in those private moments when we are simply trying to make sense of our faith for our own satisfaction, when we allow those inevitable doubts and difficulties to come to the surface of consciousness, we are engaged somehow in the enterprise of theology.

In other words, as soon as we start thinking and talking about our Christian faith, we are doing theology. And how can Christian faith exist at all if we never think or speak about it?

Every written or spoken expression of the faith is a work of theology. It is never a matter of pure faith. Thus, the sermon given from the pulpit on Sunday is not the direct Word of God. It is the preacher's own interpretation of that Word. His interpretation is theological. In preparing his sermon, he has wrestled with the problem of understanding the Christian faith, and he has tried to express that understanding with the help of certain traditional instruments: Bible commentaries, pertinent Church doctrines, creeds, theology textbooks, and other homiletical materials.

The same would be true of the doctrines and dogmas proposed by the Church. These official statements are not the pure Word of God either. They represent an attempt on the part of the college of bishops—with the special assistance of the Holy Spirit, to be sure—to express in language their own collective interpretation of the Word of God as it might apply to a particular point of discussion and controversy. Just like the preacher, they, too, make use of various traditional instruments: biblical exegesis, creeds, the writings of the Fathers, the teachings of the earlier councils, the works of certain theologians, and so forth.

This process applies also to the Bible itself, even though we have always referred to it as the very

"Word of God." Both Old and New Testaments are written interpretations of the presence of God as experienced by Israel and later by the primitive Church. We have every reason to speak of the "theology" of St. John, of Pauline "theology," and so forth. Notice, however, that I am not suggesting that the various books of the Bible are no more authoritative than the theologies of the Fathers, or of the great theologians of past and present ages. The Holy Spirit is engaged in the composition of Sacred Scripture in a way that has no parallel. We refer to the Scriptures, in fact, as the *inspired* Word of God.

The point is this: we are not addressed by a pure, unalloyed Word of God. We do not see God as he is in himself; neither do we hear his Word, as it is *in itself*. Every generation has to reinterpret constantly the interpretations of previous generations, whether these be biblical generations of Old and New Testaments, or the patristic generations, or the medieval generations, or even the generation immediately preceding our own.

We do no real service by merely repeating the old formulae. We must always ask the question: what do these statements and creeds really mean? And that question is, at root, the question of theology.

Faith, as we said at the outset of this section, cannot exist without theology. Our task is to see to it that we are using the best theologies available, because

75

it is God's own Word that we are striving not only to understand and articulate, but to live by as well.

2. Theology or Ideology?

Five or ten years ago a theologian might have been put down as an "intellectual navel-gazer" if he spent any significant amount of space on the question, "What is theology?" An impatient reader would have insisted, "Let's get on with it! Discuss the basic issues: Christ, the Trinity, redemption, grace, heaven, sin, sacraments, infallibility."

There was a widespread assumption among Catholics that the theologian's task is relatively clear-cut: to explain the teachings of the Church to each succeeding generation. The theologian should be able to do this in such a way that the older generation, if it happened to be listening in, could easily recognize what was being said and could readily nod with quiet approval.

In one sense, this concept of theology is correct. Doctrines, after all, do not stand in solitary splendor. They are part of the historical fabric of the Church and cannot be understood except as a piece of the whole garment. Therefore, to explain fully the doctrines of the Church is to explain the core of Christian tradition.

But this was not what many Catholics had in mind. They wanted the theologian to adhere almost exclusively to the doctrinal formulations themselves and to accept them at "face value" (read: according to the explanations offered by a single, approved school of theology which dominated the Catholic Church throughout the first half of this century).

These Catholics assumed that there can be only one theology and one supporting philosophy. The Christian faith is so intimately bound to these that the substitution of another theology or another philosophy would be tantamount to replacing the faith itself.

Since the unity of the Church rests upon unity of belief, it was considered absolutely essential that theologians should defend against all attack the stated doctrines of the Church. To the extent that all Catholics accept the same formulations of faith, to that same extent are all Catholics united.

The primary concern here seemed to be with the preservation of unity and harmony within the community rather than with the intrinsic truth or meaning of the doctrine or article of faith.

However, when truth serves only a unifying function within a given group, class, or culture, it becomes "ideology." Theology is not ideology, of course, but many Catholics have tended to equate the two in the past.

This leads to a brief consideration of a second assumption about the nature and task of theology; namely, that real theology (as opposed to ideology) should not be given to the so-called "simple faithful."

77

Who are the "simple faithful"? Presumably they are the Catholics who are intellectually and emotionally capable of doing only what they are told to do and of believing only what they are told to believe. All explanations and criticisms which do not rely upon the force of authority are supposedly above and beyond their mental and psychological powers.

I don't know how many Catholics would like to be placed in this category, but there seem to be enough other Catholics around who, in the name of Church unity, would like to do it for them.

This latter group recognizes that if theology is more than ideology, i.e., if it is critical and scientific, then the traditional cohesiveness of the Church is threatened. The first and most far-reaching effect of the scientific process is the undermining of belief based on authority. To investigate beliefs scientifically is to open human beings up to the possibility of feeling and acting differently.

The critical approach likewise tends to modify the privileged position of those who claim special access to authoritative truth. If one no longer accepts something just because someone in authority says it is true, then, to that same extent, the power of the authority-figure is diminished. To that same extent, again, the social cohesiveness of the group is weakened.

Accordingly, the theologian is asked to back off from his critical inquiry for the sake of the "simple faithful" when, in fact, it is for the sake of the co-hesiveness of the religious group.

I should not want to dismiss the concern for Church unity. But the end never justifies the means. Theology cannot be pressured into becoming ideology for the sake of Catholic peace and tranquility. There are other paths to that goal: the Eucharist, the sacra-ments, fraternal charity, the pastoral ministry of pope, bishops, and priests, and so forth. Theology has a different task.

3. Can Faith Exist Without Theology?

It is generally accepted that theology cannot exist without faith. We must think we have experienced the reality of God before we can begin talking about our experience. And that is precisely what theology is all about: talking about our presumed experience of God.

It is not always understood, however, that faith itself cannot exist without theology. If we never re-flect upon our experience of God, then, for all practi-cal purposes, that experience is nonexistent. As soon as we begin thinking about our presumed experience of God, we are involved in the task of theology.

Thus, while it is true that theology cannot exist without faith, it is also true that faith cannot exist without theology. Indeed, every expression of faith, even a dogmatic definition of the Church, is itself a work of theology. It is an attempt to express in language our presumed perception of God in this or that sector of life and history.

If faith cannot exist without theology, there can be no "pure faith" existing anywhere, even in the official teachings of the Church. These doctrinal pronouncements are themselves conditioned by the cultural, political, intellectual, and subjective situation in which they were written.

I do not mean to imply that the official teachings of the Church carry no more weight than, let us say, the private, scholarly opinions of an individual theologian. The college of bishops, especially when assembled in ecumenical council, has a magisterial role which is different from that of theologians and other members of the Church. The episcopal college, including the pope, has an irreplaceable function with the Body of Christ. The bishops cannot abdicate their responsibility for the unity and mission of the Church, nor can they hand it over to some other group within the Church.

But the same applies to theologians. They, too, have a distinctive ministry within the Church. They are charged, among other things, with testing the present preaching, teaching, catechesis, spirituality, and missionary activity of the Church against the abiding tradition of the Church, whether expressed in Sacred Scripture, the Fathers, the documents of earlier councils, or the writings of the important theologians of the past.

The theologians' task is different from the task of the college of bishops. Their function, too, is irreplaceable and cannot be abdicated or handed over to some other group within the Church, including even the college of bishops itself.

A tension will always exist within the Church: institutional elements versus charismatic elements, word versus sacrament, authority versus freedom, episcopal (and papal) magisterium versus the witness of theologians, and so forth.

These tensions are not inimical to the life and work of the Church. They are an essential part of her nature. The mystery of the Church is rooted in the most basic tension between the divine and the human. An incarnational community has to be a community of tension.

All of this is in response to a recent charge that the "confusion and contradiction" in the Catholic Church today is the fault of theologians, especially those "well-known" theologians who really have no faith.

We have been reminded that theology is not the faith. Theology, we are told, is affected by various circumstances, while the faith comes directly from God and its content is presented in the official teachings of the Church.

The major assumption here (and I shall not comment on the rash judgment that some of the Catholic Church's leading theologians are men without faith) is that faith is really available in pure and undiluted form in the dogmatic statements of the Church, as if these doctrinal formulations were not subject to cultural, political, and subjective human conditioning.

This is simply not true. Every expression of faith is already a theological expression. Doctrinal expressions are no exception. They depend on specific interpretations of the Bible, of the Fathers of the Church, of previous conciliar teaching, particular readings of the "signs of the times," and so forth.

I do not say that doctrinal statements have no greater authority than the statements of individual theologians or even of groups of theologians. I am saying only that faith does not exist in pure, unconditioned form.

Every expression of faith is a theological expression. We cannot have faith without theology. There is no place where faith exists by itself—not even in the textual wonderland of Denzinger.

4. Orthodoxy and Orthopraxis

We believe that it is the Holy Spirit which makes the Church one (1 Cor. 12), but how do we test the presence of the unifying Spirit? How can we tell when a Christian has a proper relationship to the Holy Spirit? How do we know that we really do participate in the one fellowship of Christ's Body, a fellowship brought together and sustained by the Spirit?

Some Catholics would say that it is a matter of common belief, of common profession of the same faith. We know we are one, they suggest, because we can express our faith in the same way and even with the same words. Those who do not believe as we do cannot be regarded as part of that same unity given by the Spirit.

Orthodoxy is the commitment to right teaching (literally: "right praise"). A Catholic is orthodox when he explicitly accepts the teachings of the Church, i.e., when his words, attitudes, and opinions conform to the official statements of the magisterium.

The opposite of orthodoxy is heresy. A Catholic is a heretic when he denies a solemn and authoritative teaching of the Church.

Many Catholics would say, even today, that the unity of the Church is manifested and preserved by orthodoxy, i.e., by common acceptance of the same teachings of the Church. For such Catholics, theological criticism of doctrines and other magisterial statements is the greatest threat to the unity of the Church. If we do not agree upon what there is to believe, then we cannot possibly be one community in the Holy Spirit.

That is why it is important to exercise censorship or at least close control over what is proposed for public consumption in the Church. And that is also why, they would argue, we need an infallible teaching authority: to protect the whole Church from the confusion and contradiction sown by the critics.

There are other Catholics who say that our unity is expressed by right practice rather than by right belief. We know we are one, they suggest, because we act in the same way. Those who do not act in the same way cannot be regarded as part of that same unity given by the Spirit.

This second group is interested in orthopraxis (literally: "right practice") rather than orthodoxy. A Catholic is orthopractic when he actively fulfills the mandate of the Gospel, i.e., when he ministers to the blind, the deaf, the sick, the dying, the persecuted, the poor, the homeless, and so forth.

The opposite of orthopraxis is hypocrisy. A Catholic is a hypocrite when he gives only lip-service to the teachings of Jesus, but in fact refuses to put that teaching into practice, all the while insisting that he still believes in it. They point especially to the twenty-fifth chapter of St. Matthew's Gospel where we see the Lord judging us not on the basis of what we believe but rather on the basis of what we have done, or failed to do.

Many Catholics would say, particularly today, that the unity of the Church is manifested and preserved by orthopraxis, i.e., by common, active commitment to the Gospel of Jesus Christ. For such Catholics, the failure of various other Christians to put the Gospel into practice is the greatest threat to the unity of the Church. If we do not share a common commitment to justice, peace, freedom, and brotherhood, then we cannot possibly be one community in the Holy Spirit.

That is why it is important today to criticize the financial and administrative operations of the Church and to challenge the religious rhetoric of those fellow Christians who have no real intention of ever putting the Gospel into practice. Prophecy is the order of the day: the prophetic criticism of both society and Church.

Both views are right; and both are wrong. The unity of the Church and, ultimately, the effectiveness of its mission are manifested and safeguarded by neither orthodoxy nor orthopraxis alone.

Against the orthodoxists, we can indeed cite the twenty-fifth chapter of St. Matthew's Gospel and also the whole social doctrine of the Catholic Church, particularly the great social encyclicals and the Pastoral Constitution on the Church in the Modern World. A Church without social and political responsibility, however ideologically pure it might be, is a Church without fidelity to the mission of Jesus Christ.

Against the orthopraxists, we must say that it is the common belief in the Lordship of Jesus which makes the Church a distinctive community in the first place. If right belief (orthodoxy) is unimportant, then the Church loses its distinctive identity.

"A church can be a missionary church only if it can say what unifies and animates it," Karl Rahner has written. "The churches can perform their service to the world together only if they can show the world that they perform their service because of a common conviction of faith against which this common action of the church can be measured even by the world itself."

DISCUSSION QUESTIONS

1. Do you think that only theologians should become bishops? If so, why? If not, why not?

2. The theologian is to the Magisterium of the Church as _____ is to the President of the United States. Would you insert the name of the President's press secretary, or a cabinet official, or a distinguished columnist for *The New York Times*, or whom? Explain your reasons for inserting some names and excluding others.

3. It is always said that theology cannot exist without faith. What does that mean to you? In this chapter I have reversed that proposition and have suggested that neither can faith exist without theology. Do you understand the importance of that statement? What practical implications does it have?

4. A leading Church official has said that his committee or congregation will not judge new theo-

logical ideas by the standard of a single Roman theology but rather by the standard of revelation. Do you think that this is really possible? If not, why not? If so, where is such "revelation" available?

5. Do you think that the Bible is the very Word of God? If so, what do you mean by that description of this religious literature? What did God do to make it his book? If you do not regard the Bible as the Word of God, why do you give it any importance at all? Do you think that the Bible is more authoritative for understanding Christian faith than, let us say, the writings of St. Thomas Aquinas or the documents of an ecumenical council? If so, why? If not, why not?

6. Do many of the Catholics you know still think that Protestants interpret Sacred Scripture by arbitrary, subjectivistic standards, while Catholics accept the objective norm imposed by the teaching authority of the Church? Do you see any difference at all today in the way Catholics and Protestants read and interpret the Bible? Are you opposed to, or in favor of, the so-called common Bible?

7. What is ideology? Can you give some examples of an ideological position that is presented in the guise of a theological position?

8. Do you think that the Catholic Church has been more interested in "right belief" than in "right

practice"? Do you think that the balance is now swinging in the other direction and that we are now in danger of suppressing belief entirely?

4

Scripture and Tradition

1. Tradition

Some Catholics may have the impression that the hierarchy of the Church has special access to a treasure chest of doctrines which has been "in the family" from the earliest days. The pope and bishops alone know fully what's in the strongbox, and it is their job, more than anyone else's, to defend its contents against all who would dare to steal or destroy them.

This is, in fact, still a common way of referring to the various elements of Christian faith, and so it is no wonder that many Catholics continue to think of religious truths in this way. For example, Pope Paul VI, in his opening address before the first meeting of the International Theological Commission in Rome, urged the members present to "defend the people of God from the numerous, excessive, and pressing errors that are assailing the *divine deposit of truth*" (emphasis mine).

This highly objective, and almost static, understanding of Christian tradition has its origin, at least partially, in the wording of certain decrees of the Council of Trent (and later the First Vatican Council). When the Fathers of Vatican II came to write article 7 of the Dogmatic Constitution on Divine

Revelation, they consciously based their text on a similar passage in the documents of Trent.

Several commentators, including Karl Rahner's colleague, Joseph Ratzinger, have called attention to the various subtle, but significant, changes that Vatican II made in the Tridentine text.

Whereas Trent spoke only of the "promulgation" of the Gospel by Christ (as if the Gospel were a matter of legalities), Vatican II adds the word "*adimplevit*": "Christ himself *fulfilled* (the Gospel) and promulgated it with his own lips."

Secondly, whereas Trent spoke of Christ as commissioning the Apostles to preach the Gospel to all men as the source of all saving truth and moral teaching, Vatican II adds the phrase: "and thus to communicate to them divine gifts." Tradition, therefore, is not simply a matter of handing on official doctrines proposed and defined in some earlier period of the Church's history. It is a matter of grace and dialogue ("*communicare . . . dona*").

But this understanding of Tradition changes its usual meaning. If the origin of Tradition is not merely the promulgation of laws which are to be passed on to succeeding generations, then the very idea of "passing on" has to be reevaluated. It must mean something different.

Thirdly, Trent taught that the starting-point of Tradition is the preaching of Christ and the preaching of the Apostles. Again, according to this notion, the "handing on" of Christian faith is a matter of carefully repeating and interpreting the original statements of the Lord and the leaders of the primitive Church.

But Vatican II adds something more: "This commission was faithfully fulfilled by the apostles who, by their oral preaching, by example, and by pastoral practices, handed on what they received . . ." Tradition is not only a matter of transmitting the Gospel by word of mouth. The Gospel is communicated to subsequent generations through the whole life-style and Christian example of the early Church.

Finally, whereas the Council of Trent had spoken of the Holy Spirit as "dictating" what was to be handed on, Vatican II speaks of the "prompting" or the "suggestion" of the Spirit. The idea of dictation implies that Tradition is a matter of communicating the Gospel through precise legal decrees and doctrinal statements; the idea of "prompting" implies that there is more to Tradition than the transmission of formulae.

The preceding paragraphs may appear a bit more technical than necessary. But it should be made clear that important changes and advances are not usually grasped "on the run." Vatican II does not stand in a vacuum, and its documents are not in the category of pious exhortation. They are carefully drawn, and only a careful analysis makes it possible to understand their significance. And understanding the significance of Vatican II is, after all, a necessary first step to understanding what has been happening in the Church over the last several years.

2. Tradition and Traditions

The word "Tradition" means more than the "deposit of faith." The Dogmatic Constitution on Divine Revelation expanded its meaning significantly beyond what had been proposed at the Council of Trent. A Catholic, therefore, does not do full justice to the notion of Tradition when he refers to it as "the sum total of revealed truths found outside of Sacred Scripture."

Rather, Tradition has to do with the multi-dimensional presence of Christ in the Church. I realize that this sentence is not self-explanatory. It has the ring of theological jargon. What does it mean?

The Church is, in a very special way, the visible presence of Christ in the world. St. Paul used the expression "Body of Christ." St. Augustine, and other Fathers of the Church, called the Church a "sacrament" of Christ. Contemporary theologians, such as Rahner and Schillebeeckx, have offered sophisticated definitions of both terms, especially the latter.

The Church, as the sacrament of Christ, i.e., the visible sign of his redemptive presence in history, embodies Christ in various ways: in its teachings, doctrines, liturgies, sacraments, customs, and in its over-all style of life in the world. When the Church reflects on this multi-dimensional presence of Christ throughout its whole history, it is engaged in the task of consulting Tradition, of measuring her contemporary activity against the background of her origins and past experiences.

This is not, of course, the understanding of Tradition that prevailed earlier in this century, and even at the time of the council itself. The conventional view identified Tradition with certain extrabiblical truths of faith, uncovered and proclaimed authoritatively by the Church. Vatican II widened this concept to include not only teachings but also worship and pastoral practice.

Undoubtedly, this broader definition is superior to the earlier concept, but it is not without difficulties of its own. According to article 8 of *Dei Verbum*, Tradition embraces the total life of the Church, but the text does not provide any critical principles whereby the contemporary Church can discern the good from the bad, the essential from the accidental, in its own past.

How do we separate the authentic Tradition of the Church from those "traditions" which are not only eminently dispensable but even harmful and distorting? This was precisely the question raised by the late Cardinal Meyer of Chicago, at the beginning of the council's third session (September 30, 1964).

While Tradition may be broader in scope than the Bible, he noted, the living tradition of the Church

93

is not always free of human defects. The Church, after all, is a pilgrim community. It has not yet attained the perfection Christ promised it. It would be an exaggeration, therefore, to speak of Tradition as if the Church were involved in a process of continual improvement.

As examples where the traditions of the Church (and the word "traditions" is purposely placed in the lower case) have deviated from the Tradition of the Church, he cited the exaggerated moralism of past centuries, private pious practices which have grown away from the spirit of the liturgy, neglect of the Bible, and even the active discouragement of Bible reading among Catholics that occurred in certain areas.

He concluded with the reminder that such defects are always possible, and insisted that the Bible must serve as a corrective norm by which these traditions (and, therefore, Tradition itself) can be judged.

The problem of Tradition and traditions is hardly a matter of academic interest alone. Catholics who have been involved in the struggle for reform and renewal, in parishes, seminaries, colleges, religious communities, dioceses, or even at the international level, have found that Tradition and traditions are sometimes confused and that opposition to change, or defense of long-standing customs and practices, often arises from a failure to see the difference.

94

The eighth article of *Dei Verbum* has not completely solved this problem, but it has at least provided some useful principles within which the discussion can be carried on.

3. *Scripture and Tradition*

What is the relationship between Scripture and Tradition? To most readers the question probably sounds very academic. Those with longer and sharper memories will know that the issue was a point of major controversy in the earlier stages of the Second Vatican Council, so much so that there was a general belief that the council would never produce a document on divine revelation.

However, the controversy cooled sufficiently to make such a document possible. The Dogmatic Constitution on Divine Revelation, known by its Latin title as *Dei Verbum*, was passed and promulgated within a month of the council's final adjournment. The pertinent material on the Scripture-and-Tradition question is contained in articles nine and ten.

I should suggest that the discussion was not merely academic. There have been various misconceptions about the meaning of Scripture, Tradition, and their specific interrelationship, and these misconceptions have affected the way in which Christians understand and practice their faith. To the extent that the issue impinges upon Catholic belief and life, to that same extent does the Scripture-and-Tradition question assume eminently practical dimensions.

Lutheran theologian George A. Lindbeck, of Yale University, regards this problem as the principal ecumenical issue dividing Catholics from Protestants (see his *The Future of Roman Catholic Theology,* Fortress Press, 1970, esp. chapter V). And Father Gregory Baum has insisted that the Roman Catholic Church's distinctive strength is its peculiar ability to bridge the gap between present experience and past formulations of faith, particularly the classic formulations of Sacred Scripture (see his *The Credibility of the Church Today,* Herder and Herder, 1968, chapter IV, and *Faith and Doctrine,* Newman Press, 1970, chapter III).

What are some of the common misunderstandings of Scripture, of Tradition, and of their specific interrelationship?

(1) Many Christians (especially Protestants) tend to identify the Word of God exclusively with Sacred Scripture, in the sense that only the Bible contains Revelation. Tradition is of no ultimate, intrinsic value.

(2) Many other Christians (mostly Roman Catholics) have tended to look upon Tradition as a separate and distinct source of Revelation, a source that might be considered wholly independent of, if not superior to, Sacred Scripture.

(3) There are also some Christians who, while not regarding Tradition as independent of, or superior to, the Bible, look upon Tradition simply as

the *post*biblical interpretation of the Word of God. Thus, Scripture and Tradition are two closely related, but essentially separate, realities. The Bible is the Word of God insofar as it has been committed to writing under the inspiration of the oly Spirit, and Tradition is the Spirit-directed reflection upon that written Word, after the fact.

What is to be said about these common assumptions? Does the Dogmatic Constitution on Divine Revelation provide any guidance?

(1) Although the Roman Catholic community itself suffered for a brief time (roughly the period of the late 1950's and early 1960's) from the temptation of biblicism (which means the tendency to regard all theology as biblical theology and all revelation as biblical revelation), this first position cannot claim any serious support either in contemporary Catholic theology or in the documents of Vatican II.

Dei Verbum makes it clear, for example, that revelation is not a matter of words alone, but of events as well, and particularly the event of Jesus Christ (articles 2-4). Consequently, when we say that we must judge everything according to the Gospel, we do not mean only "the Book" but also the living expression of that Gospel in the history and experience of the Church.

(2) The idea that Scripture and Tradition are two separate and independent sources of revelation (with the implication that Tradition is superior to the Bible

because it judges it and interprets it for later generations) possessed considerable influence in the Catholic theological community for some time, particularly during the first half of this century. However, Vatican II chose not to endorse this notion, deciding instead to leave the question open (see articles 9 and 10, and also the still valuable study by Brother Gabriel Moran, *Scripture and Tradition: A Survey of the Controversy,* Herder and Herder, 1963).

(3) The third notion is closer to the truth and therefore more difficult to criticize. This will be the concern of the remainder of this chapter.

There have been two extreme views on the question of Scripture-and-Tradition, and the Second Vatican Council has rejected both of them.

The *first view* equates Revelation with the Bible. God's Word is a written word, inspired by the Holy Spirit. Postbiblical Tradition, whether written or unwritten, can have no final claim upon our faith.

This is the view of the many so-called "Bible Christians," particularly those of the various fundamentalist sects. Theirs is a religion of the Book. Sacred Scripture is a collection of truths directly revealed by God. It is the source of all truth and the basis of all life.

The insistence of its partisans notwithstanding, the Bible is not a simple book to read and to understand. Without some appreciation of the process by which it was written, its cultural and historical setting, the meaning of its language and concepts, and so forth, the casual reader is not going to derive the full benefit of its content. On the contrary, many will read and interpret the Bible in seemingly contradictory ways, or in ways that appear to conflict with the Church's own understanding of the Gospel (e.g., the use of the Bible to justify racial segregation).

Not all Christians who identify Revelation with the Bible are fundamentalists, of course. But those Christians who do make their faith a matter of fidelity to a book tend also to make Christianity an essentially past-oriented reality. Being a Christian means to remember what God said to us many centuries ago and then to remain faithful to his words to the extent that we can. History, whether of the present or of the future, has nothing new to tell us. God terminated his monologue at the death of the last of the Apostles.

Vatican II declared, on the other hand, that God reveals himself through history itself, and not only through words (*Dei Verbum,* arts. 2-4). And Sacred Scripture is itself produced by the convergence of several different traditions (art. 19).

The council also recognized that God draws near even to those who are not in the Judaeo-Christian tradition (see the Dogmatic Constitution on the Church, art. 16). His Word is not confined to the Hebrew or the Christian Scriptures, and neither can the vision of the Christian community be confined to the past (see, for example, the Pastoral Constitution on the Church in the Modern World, art. 39).

The *second view* implies that Tradition (i.e., non-biblical revelation) is independent of, if not superior to, Sacred Scripture. The Bible can have no meaning for us unless it is properly interpreted, and that "proper" interpretation is provided by the Church. The successive interpretations of the Bible comprise the Tradition, although Tradition is not limited to biblical interpretation alone. There are some items of revelation (e.g., the seven sacraments, certain Mariological doctrines, the determination of the canon of Sacred Scripture) which are not contained in the Bible itself.

The Second Vatican Council refused to reaffirm this view, even though many Catholic theologians before and during the council had assumed that this was the only correct position. The Dogmatic Constitution on Divine Revelation left the question open, insisting only that "sacred tradition and sacred Scripture form one sacred deposit of the word of God, which is committed to the Church" (art. 10).

Furthermore, the council taught that the teaching authority of the Church has not been set *above* the Bible as its official interpreter and judge. Rather, this teaching office "serves" the Word of God, "teaching only what has been handed on, listening to it devoutly, guarding it scrupulously, and explaining it faithfully by divine commission and with the help of the Holy Spirit . . ." (art. 10).

But what about the *third view,* which looks upon Scripture and Tradition as two closely related, but separate, realities? It seems to avoid the weaknesses of both extremes: it refuses to identify revelation exclusively with the Bible, and yet it acknowledges that the Church's reflections must be tied essentially to the biblical expression of the primitive faith.

This third view, despite its obvious superiority over the first two notions, assumes that Sacred Scripture alone conveys to us the Word of God in pure and undistilled form. The view tends to place the Bible in a category so separate and distinct that we begin to conclude that the writing of Old and New Testaments did not involve the same processes that are involved in the development of theology, the formulation of doctrines and creeds, the production of liturgy, and so forth.

This is not the case. Scripture and Tradition should not be distinguished too sharply. Indeed, Scripture is itself a form and an expression of Tradition.

The Bible is not the pure Word of God in the sense that God himself physically wrote the Bible or dictated its contents to certain handpicked writers. There have been notions of Biblical inspiration that have approved the dictation view, but these have never been accepted officially by the Church. Indeed, such ideas create more theological problems than they resolve.

If the Bible is not the Word of God in the sense indicated above, how can it be called his Word at all? It may come as something of a surprise to learn that this question has been very much an open one. (For the most recent survey of the discussion within the Roman Catholic community, see James T. Burtchaell's *Catholic Theories of Biblical Inspiration Since 1810,* Cambridge University Press, 1969.)

The discussion hinges upon the solution to several related problems: the meaning of revelation, the nature and quality of understanding that is given by faith, the relationship between faith and its verbal formulations, and so forth.

What must be clear is that the Bible is not a collection of books given from on high in exactly the form we now have them. The Bible is the work of communities of faith, and of individuals within those communities: first of Israel, and then of the primitive Christian Church.

What we have in the Bible are the written expressions of what the authors (whether individuals or groups of individuals) assumed to be the inbreaking of God in their experience and in their history. The authors of Sacred Scripture did not actually *see* God acting; they saw people and events which they *interpreted* to be the action of God in the world.

The Bible, then, contains the various interpreta-

tions of both the Israelite and the Christian perceptions of God's presence in history. When we study
the Bible, we are studying the interpretations of
divine action as mediated through the faith of Israel
and the early Church.

These interpretations, however, are not on the
same level with the writings of a given theologian,
nor even of an ecumenical council of the Church.
Since these interpretations were formulated in the
period of primitive establishment, i.e., in that period
when the Church was coming into being, they have
a special authority that cannot be duplicated by any
later text.

We might use the analogy of the Constitution of
the United States. This document was produced by
the Founding Fathers of this country and all later
political literature would simply have to come to
terms with it. Either the nation remains faithful to
the original ideas upon which it was founded, or it
decides to become something else entirely. So long
as it is determined to remain what it has been, the
country accords special reverence and attention to
what is contained in its initial constitutional decree.

God is the author of Sacred Scripture in the sense
that he is the author of the Church. And to the extent that he intended the Church to commit to writing its initial insights of faith, to that same extent
did he will the production of its Sacred Scripture.
This is basically the argument advanced by Karl

Rahner, S.J., in his extraordinarily influential work, *Inspiration in the Bible* (Herder and Herder, 1964).

In one sense, therefore, the Bible is "privileged theology." It is the primitive community's written interpretation of its perception of God's transforming presence in and through Jesus of Nazareth. If we believe that the Church itself is a work of the Holy Spirit, gathering men from every land and nation, then we should be prepared to affirm that the Church's normative literature is also a work of that same Holy Spirit, not merely in the sense that the Spirit is involved in all good works, but in a special, even unique, sense. The Bible is inspired in a manner that no other writing, sacred or otherwise, is inspired (see *Dei Verbum*, chapter III).

Is it really sufficient, however, to say that Scripture and Tradition are two separate expressions of divine revelation, in such wise that Tradition is merely the faithful interpretation of Scripture?

When the Bible is understood in this other, larger sense, it becomes clear that Scripture and Tradition are a part of the same basic process whereby a community of faith attempts to express its perception of God. Sacred Scripture is that special segment of the Tradition-process whereby the insights of the *primitive* community are committed to writing and thereby become a norm of all later insights and interpretations.

DISCUSSION QUESTIONS

1. What was your understanding of "tradition" before reading this chapter? Do you think that the distinction between "Tradition and traditions" is an important one? Can you think of any unfortunate consequences that have occurred because of a misunderstanding of this distinction?

2. What is the relationship between Scripture and Tradition? Do you think that this question has any real relevance to the problem we are treating in this book; namely, what does it mean to be a Catholic? If not, why not? If so, why?

5

Magisterium and Dissent

1. The Pope, the Bishops, and Contemporary Theology

It may seem that each time the pope or the bishops speak out on some doctrinal issue they are smothered with criticism from certain quarters in the Church. Cardinal Heenan complained recently in the *London Tablet* that bishops are afraid to question new theological views lest they be dismissed as reactionaries and their authority weakened still further.

This may be true in many instances, particularly where the bishop is aware of his own theological inadequacies and finds himself in a diocese or region that is without suitable academic resources. Most bishops realize today that one does not consult a canon lawyer or a philosopher (or worse: someone with no academic credentials whatever) to determine the validity of new views in contemporary theology.

What is the alternative? Are the pope and the bishops to stand by like silent spectators as the Church makes its own faltering way into the future? If they did this, they would justifiably be criticized for abdicating their responsibilities as leaders and spokesmen for the entire Christian community.

The resolution of this apparent dilemma must somehow overcome both criticisms. The pope and the bishops must reassert their historic roles as symbols of unity and as the principal spokesmen for the authentic tradition of the Church, especially in a time of pronounced change such as our own. But they cannot confuse this tradition with the arguments and conclusions of the theological textbooks in use during the first half of this century. The authentic tradition is embodied in Sacred Scripture, in the major doctrinal interventions of the Church, and in the present living experience of the Christian community. It is the joint task of the magisterium, the theologians, and of the whole Church, to whom the Spirit has been given, to discern and to disclose this tradition for each new age.

This means that the pope and the bishops must encourage, promote, and financially support good theological research, writing, and education at every level in the Church: from the catechetical enterprise in the home, the grade school, and the high school, to the academic pursuits of the university and the seminary. It means initiating and sustaining the kind of research projects that are common in modern business and industry and placing a higher value on scientific exploration not only in theology but in its various related fields.

Communication and collaboration must characterize the day-to-day relationship between bishop and theologian: the theologian needs this if he is to appreciate better the delicate pastoral situation in which he does his work; and the bishop needs this if he is to understand and properly evaluate that situation in the light of the best theology that is available.

The same kind of dialogue must obtain between bishop and theologian, on the one hand, and the total Christian community, on the other—for reasons which are too obvious to enumerate. Such dialogue will serve, in part, to dramatize the urgent need for serious and imaginative adult religious education. In its absence, the Church will continue to drift for several more decades in a mood of confusion and frustration.

It would border on the irresponsible to suggest that failing grades are to be assigned across the board for past performances. The bishops have sponsored several important research projects, and many of the theologians who enjoy the freedom to criticize the Church were themselves educated at Church expense. Furthermore, bishops and theologians have cooperated on various common projects, most notably the Second Vatican Council itself, and both groups have been influenced by their widening contacts with the larger Christian community. The point is, as the late Senator Kennedy used to say, "We can do better."

Thus far, I have spoken only of the positive tasks of the magisterium of the Church. Is there any longer a place for admonition, for questioning, for criticism of new theological views? Or is the situation which

109

Cardinal Heenan describes both necessary and permanent? Are there, in fact, any doctrinal areas which require today some kind of clear and firm magisterial reaffirmation?

There are at least three major areas of Catholic belief that require firm and consistent reaffirmation on the part of the pope, the bishops, and all others in the Church who communicate the message of the Gospel through preaching and teaching: (1) the relevance of the Gospel to the socio-political order; (2) the Lordship of Jesus Christ; and (3) the place of ministry in the Church.

The first concerns our basic *human* responsibilities; the second, our specifically *Christian* faith; and the third, our distinctively *Catholic* convictions.

What is demanded at this first level of faith is demanded of every human being: all men are called by God to live with compassion and concern for one's neighbor, even if one cannot say, "Lord, Lord!"

What is required at the second level of faith is required of every person who presumes to call himself a Christian. Not only must he live according to the Gospel, but he must confess that Jesus of Nazareth is the Lord, that he is the unique and ultimate pattern for all human life and history.

Finally, what is imposed at the third level of faith is imposed upon every Christian who regards himself as a Catholic. Insofar as he is a Christian, the Catholic is one who lives the Gospel because he is convinced of the Lordship of Jesus Christ. But the Catholic further specifies this faith by his conviction that the Christian life to which he has been called is to be lived within a definite, structured community whose cohesiveness is officially insured by the presence of the college of bishops, with the successor of Peter at its center and head.

Thus, the Catholic affirms that the ordained ministry is not simply a function within the Church but an essential aspect of the ecclesial mystery itself. And the Church is not simply a group of people sharing common social ideals, but it is the very creation of God and the Body of Christ.

- In recent years each of these three areas of Catholic belief have been the subject of some confusion, occasional flippancy, and even outright denial in certain segments of the Church—left, right, and center. The Church's leadership has not only the right but the duty to question, criticize, and at times decisively reject theological views which undermine these truths of Catholic faith. Such magisterial interventions, however, must always presuppose the kind of relationships and atmosphere that were described above, i.e., open communication and full collaboration among the bishops, the theologians, and the rest of the Church.

(1) The Gallup poll of March, 1969, which found that 57 per cent of American Catholics (and 52 per cent of American Protestants) reject the involvement

111

of the Church in matters of political or social consequence, confirmed what many religious leaders and members of the Church had already long suspected: a distressingly large number of Christians do not recognize the essential connection between the Gospel and the life of the human community. They have not yet assimilated the teaching of the council's Pastoral Constitution on the Church in the Modern World, nor the recent social encyclicals of Pope John XXIII and Pope Paul VI.

(2) There are some Christians (and it seems that a few Catholics have recently joined their ranks) who have not been clear and unequivocal about their faith in the Lordship of Jesus Christ. Any view which tends to relativize the uniqueness of the Lord, any flippancy which discounts "Jesus-talk," must move the Church to reaffirm its faith that Jesus is the norm against which all else is judged and his Gospel is the standard against which all life is measured.

(3) There is a tendency, too, among some Catholics to minimize or even to reject the place of ministry in the Church. Occasionally the rhetoric of the so-called "Underground Church" reflects this spirit. The charismatic is exalted at the expense of the structural; the tyranny of the old legalism is supplanted by a new tyranny of the spirit (with a small "s").

However, even as the Church reaffirms the essential place of ministry, it must do so within the context of the council's emphasis on ministry as service. An emphatic defense of ministerial structure is both credible and effective where the ministerial offices are being employed in the service of the Kingdom of God. When the principal concern is the preservation of the institution as such, the defense assumes a petulant and plaintive ring.

2. *The Learning Magisterium*

Few conciliar statements have been so popular with the defenders of *Humanae Vitae* as the second paragraph of article 25 in the Dogmatic Constitution on the Church. Herein, we are reminded that the teaching of the bishops on matters of faith and morals is to be accepted with "a religious assent of soul," while a "religious submission of mind and will must be shown in a special way to the authentic teaching authority of the Roman Pontiff, even when he is not speaking ex cathedra." But this text raises some questions.

Why do we insist that the college of bishops, when it includes the pope, is the supreme teaching authority in the Church, to the extent that its teaching has a solemn claim upon our minds and wills? Surely it isn't enough to say that this authority is supreme because Christ conferred it upon the Church and intended it to be accepted as such. That does not really answer the fundamental question: *how* do these official teachers come to know the content of faith which they are commissioned to pass on to the rest of the Church?

Is there a special channel of communication that God has opened between himself and the pope and the bishops? Are the principal officeholders in the Church the recipients of special private revelation, involving either visions or direct infusion of knowledge? Certainly no one in the Catholic Church believes this, and least of all the pope and the bishops.

How, then, do we know if what the pope and the bishops are teaching on a given occasion is true or false? Must we assume that they are always right? Is blind obedience the expected response? Not even the most rigidly juridical theology of the past has ever made such a claim. On the contrary, the *First* Vatican Council condemned such an attitude as "Fideism."

Is it enough to say that the magisterium of the Church is endowed with the enlightment of the Holy Spirit? The council document indicates that the pope and the bishops do, in fact, operate "under the guiding light of the Spirit of truth" when they are involved in the transmission of revelation to the whole Church (art. 25, para. 7). But does the Spirit guarantee 100 per cent accuracy? Again, not even the most rigidly juridical theologies of the past made such a claim.

The council reminds us here, as it did in the Constitution on Divine Revelation (art. 10, para. 2), that the teaching office is not above the Word of God, but serves it. The magisterium must teach not its own truth, but the truth of God's Word. But the question remains: how does the magisterium apprehend this truth? What criteria does it use, and what criteria does the Church use in evaluating the success or failure of this quest for truth?

Article 25, para. 7, insists that the pope and the bishops must "strive painstakingly and by appropriate means to inquire properly into that revelation and to give apt expression to its contents." And this is to be understood as a moral duty incumbent upon all who share in the teaching authority of the Church.

The "apt means" consist of constant recourse to Sacred Scripture, the work of biblical scholars, historians, dogmatic theologians, anthropologists, sociologists, and so forth. A consistent effort must be made to overcome the tendency to rely exclusively on one school of theology, and thereby to identify the Word of God with the opinions of that one school of thought. There must be a free and open exchange of views, living contact with the faith and "public opinion" of the whole community—institutional and charismatic, Catholic and non-Catholic, Christian and non-Christian.

Consequently, it is not enough to say that because such-and-such a doctrine has been proposed by the magisterium of the Church, every Catholic must accept it as true, with a "religious submission of mind and will." The magisterium, too, has a *learning* responsibility. It must always "strive painstakingly and

115

by appropriate means to inquire properly into that revelation and to give apt expression to its contents."

When there is evidence that this has not been done adequately, the "submission of mind and will" cannot be engaged. These "human" criteria do not exclude the "guiding light of the Spirit of truth," but in their absence, the appeal to the Spirit is both unwarranted and meaningless.

3. *The Teaching Magisterium*

A survey conducted soon after the release of Pope Paul VI's encyclical on the regulation of births disclosed that *Humanae Vitae* changed the minds of only two per cent of the American Catholic clergy. That is, among the group that had earlier favored contraception as a viable moral option, only two priests in a hundred were persuaded to return to the more "traditional" position by the papal encyclical. Indeed, a more recent survey of American priests indicates that the encyclical has actually had the opposite effect.

I have no intention to reopen the birth control controversy in this section. The deeper issue is the credibility and effectiveness of the magisterium of the Church, and the deeper question: How many minds are actually formed or changed by official documents of the Church?

How many Catholics, particularly among the affluent, have in fact changed their opinions about the stewardship of wealth in response to the social encyclicals of Pope Leo XIII, Pope Pius XI, Pope John XXIII, and Pope Paul VI?

How many Catholics, rich and poor, have actually changed their attitudes toward black people because of the American bishops' statement in 1958?

How many American Catholics have altered their political ideas about nuclear disarmament in the light of Vatican II's clear strictures against the continuation of the arms race?

How many Catholics have actually modified their understanding of the papacy because of the council's teaching on collegiality? How many, despite this teaching, still look upon the pope as a kind of absolute monarch?

How many Catholics abandoned their fundamentalist attitude in the interpretation of Sacred Scripture precisely because of Pope Pius XII's encyclical *Divino Afflante Spiritu* (1943), or the decree of the Pontifical Biblical Commission (1964), or the Constitution on Divine Revelation of the Second Vatican Council (1965)?

How many Catholic institutions (parishes, hospitals, schools, etc.) have raised salaries, extended fringe benefits, or encouraged the formation of unions in specific response to one of the many documents containing the social teachings of the Church?

How many Catholics changed their emotional and political attitudes toward war and violence as a solution to social and economic problems, just because of Pope Paul VI's dramatic speech before the United Nations in 1965?

Indeed, how many Catholics have actually read (in whole or in substantial part) any of the social encyclicals, any of the council documents, any of the pastoral letters of the American bishops, any of the decrees emanating from the Roman offices, or any of the speeches of the incumbent pope or his immediate predecessors?

One has only to attempt such a reading to see why the official and quasi-official teachings of the Church receive little more than casual attention (and much of the attention they *do* receive seems to spring from the curiosity of the secular press about the human power struggles that often surround the publication of such documents). Written in a style that is often a pale imitation of diplomatic rhetoric or court prose, magisterial texts are so florid, cumbersome, and strategically subtle as to become practically unintelligble for the average reader. The confusion and diversity of interpretation following the American bishops' statement on the birth control question (even among some of the bishops themselves) is a case in point.

In this time of rapid change and sharp, open debate in the Catholic Church, several of its members have come rushing forward to the defense of the magisterium, insisting all the while that a Church without an infallible and binding doctrinal authority is a Church without moorings, without certainty, without security. But one has a right to wonder which world such Catholics are describing: the abstract world of early 20th-century Catholic textbooks, or the factual world of mid 20th-century human experience?

There is, indeed, a crisis of authority in the Church. But the crisis does not arise primarily from the failure of Catholics to listen to and obey legitimate ecclesiastical authority. The more radical problem is how to make the officeholders themselves study, reflect, consult, speak, and act in such a way that their individual and collective doctrinal utterances are understandable, believable, and practical.

All those who care for the future of the Church must put themselves at the disposal of these officeholders in a spirit of fraternal cooperation and mutual concern for the realization of God's Kingdom. The officeholder must, in turn, seek out this help— but from the widest possible spectrum of competence and opinion that he can find. Consultation with those for whom there are no questions, only answers, will not dissolve the crisis that is upon us all.

4. Theological Dissent

The papacy is supposed to be the focal point of unity in the Church. Instead, we have seen it become in our time a source of deep and sharp division, even within the Roman Catholic community.

Catholics who have been alarmed by the movement and direction of their Church in the last few years and who are unashamedly nostalgic for the quiet days before Vatican II have made loyalty to the pope a kind of symbol of their rejection of change. And those Catholics who are less and less inclined to pursue the arduous path of reconciliation and reform (because they have, in fact, lost faith in the viability of Catholicism) have made of him a scapegoat for failure and an excuse for withdrawal.

The Second Vatican Council, at first glance, seems to be firmly on the loyalists' side. Article 25, paragraph 2, of *Lumen Gentium* indicates that Catholics must give a religious submission of mind and of will to all papal teachings, even when these teachings are not proposed as infallible. The case seems open and shut. The loyalists are right; the dissenters are wrong.

Moreover, the council document makes no provision for theological dissent against papal and/or episcopal teachings. The finally adopted text doesn't even mention the possibility, despite the fact that such dissent had been justified earlier by the so-called "traditional authors." How, then, can we make any sense of, or find any justification for, the kind of theological dissent that is very much in evidence today, particularly in the immediate aftermath of the Pope's "Credo of the People of God" and his encyclical letter, *Humanae Vitae*?

A slightly different understanding of article 25 (para. 2) emerges, however, when one studies the history of the text. The first draft (November 10, 1962) mentioned the possibility of theological dissent only to reject it without qualification. Citing Pope Pius XII's encyclical *Humani Generis* (1950), the original document read: "If the supreme pontiffs (in the ordinary magisterium) deliberately pass judgment on a matter hitherto controversial, it should be clear to all that according to the mind and will of the popes, the matter may not be further discussed publicly by theologians." It is highly significant that this directive was *not* carried over into the final text.

Nowhere does the council explicitly reject the possibility of responsible theological dissent. And yet there are Catholics today who argue as if this is, in fact, the official position of the Church. They seem to imply that once a pope has spoken, the issue is settled. Those who agree with the pope are right; those who disagree are wrong. Such an opinion, it should be clear, has no basis in the teachings of Vatican II.

Furthermore, the American bishops in their 1968 pastoral letter, "Human Life in Our Day," have specifically acknowledged the possibility of such dissent: "There exists in the Church a lawful freedom of inquiry and of thought and also general norms of licit dissent. This is particularly true in the area of legitimate theological speculation and research . . .

The reverence due all sacred matters, particularly questions which touch on salvation, will not necessarily require the responsible scholar to relinquish his opinion . . ."

In the light of the council's refusal to retain the prohibitive reference to *Humani Generis* and of the American bishops' openness to the possibility of theological dissent, it is difficult to see how any Catholic can continue to argue, *a priori*, that such dissent is simply wrong and can never be justified.

But some important questions remain: (1) Are there any limitations to this freedom of dissent? (2) Does the theologian have any special responsibility toward the larger community of the Church when expressing such dissent? (3) Is the possibility of such dissent limited strictly to professional theologians, i.e., those with graduate degrees in theology and teaching positions in recognized theologates? (4) If theological dissent is possible where can it be expressed? Must the theologian restrict his publications on controversial matters to the so-called scholarly journal, or does he have a right and/or a responsibility to make his reflections available to a larger reading public.

Judging by the quality and kind of opinions which the 1968 presidential campaign elicited from a large portion of the American citizenry, one might conclude that there are any number of people who would not support the Bill of Rights were it proposed today

122

in a general referendum. They would certainly want to strike those items which provide protection for the individual against the inordinate (and sometimes ordinary) use of police power, and they would want to minimize or seriously curtail the right of due process.

There have been many psychological and sociological studies into the nature and character of the rigid and authoritarian personality. I am not aware of any scientific conclusion, derived from these studies, which would necessarily and consistently link these personality traits with one's religious convictions. On the contrary, the attitudes one displays in the area of religion often reflect one's antecedent psychological makeup and sociological background, education, and experiences.

I am suggesting hereby that the views of various Catholics on the propriety (or even the possibility) of theological dissent against papal or episcopal teachings should not be regarded automatically as a reflection of their deepest religious convictions. Accordingly, the defender of the pope is not automatically a man of deep faith, extraordinary humility, and authentic holiness, nor is every dissenter a man of unusual insight into the Gospel, touched in a uniquely charismatic way by the very Spirit of God.

Fortunately, the American bishops in their recent pastoral letter, "Human Life in Our Day," avoided every kind of "motivational research" on this question and tried to present the issue with some measure of objectivity. They argued that theological dissent by professional theologians is, indeed, possible and proper, even when it is levelled against explicit statements of the pope and/or the bishops of the Church and even when the magisterium intends these statements to be binding upon the whole Church. Such dissent, however, must be exercised responsibly.

In every instance there must be "careful respect for the consciences of those who lack (the) special competence or opportunity for judicious investigation." The dissenter must have proper regard for the "gravity of the matter and (give) deference due the authority which has pronounced it," granting always an antecedent respect for that authority. The theologian should reasonably be able to assume that the magisterium has used all the apt means to reach its doctrinal or disciplinary conclusions. Such a presumption yields always to fact. Where facts to the contrary emerge, the theologian is free to call such teachings into question.

When this situation exists, the theologian must be sure that his reasons are "serious and well-founded" and he must strive to present and explain the papal or episcopal position as fairly and as accurately as possible.

These conditions for responsible theological dissent are reasonable enough. I do not think any theologian would object to any of them. But a further question arises at this point: Where can the theologian express his reservations about these teachings? Is he restricted to the professional theological journals, and preferably those which even the professional reads only sparingly? The American bishops do not say this, and I find it highly significant that they do not. There has been much pressure for precisely such a restrictive position. Some Catholics grant the right of dissent to the professional theologian—in theory— but they firmly reject his right and/or responsibility to bring this dissent to the attention of a larger reading public.

The bishops leave this question open. They admit that the development of the communications media has radically changed the character of human life. One can no longer speak realistically about purely "private" theological debate. There are no theological journals nor any professional conferences which are not accessible to the knowledgeable non-professional (i.e., the religion editors of weekly news magazines or large daily newspapers, not to mention the editors and reporters for some segments of the Catholic press).

The pastoral letter mentions this fact, not to deplore it but to respond positively to it. Nor does the American hierarchy pretend to have a ready-made formula for dealing with it; they ask for the initiation of "fruitful dialogue between bishops and theologians." The pastoral letter has no time for the usual recriminations levelled against the professional theologian. It acknowledges that both the bishops and the theologians have their diverse ministries in the Church, their distinct responsibilities to the faith and their respective charisms."

The bishops, therefore, accept the possibility and, under certain reasonable conditions, the propriety of theological dissent, even against the public, explicit, official teaching of the pope and/or the bishops. Furthermore, they do not argue in principle against the publication and dissemination of this dissent via channels other than the so-called scholarly journal. They leave the question open for further dialogue. It cannot begin soon enough.

Accordingly, it is clear that the professional theologian has the right to dissent from official papal and/or episcopal teachings. The Second Vatican Council refused to suppress this right, and the American bishops reaffirmed it openly in their pastoral letter, "Human Life in Our Day."

There are, of course, some Catholics who continue to express the opposite view from pulpits or in the letters-to-the-editor columns of the Catholic press, but they are wrong. Passion has never been an adequate substitute for scientific competence.

Which raises one final question connected with this issue of theological dissent: Is the professional theologian the only member of the Church who has the right (presumably because he alone has the competence) to dissent from official statements of the magisterium?

What about the professional sociologist whose area of research brings him again and again into confrontation with the problem of religion and its contemporary expressions? What about the philosopher whose area of study and writing has been in that border-line territory where theology and philosophy tend to converge?

What about the historian whose knowledge of the development of certain doctrines of the Church may exceed that of the professional theologian? What about the exceptionally intelligent and well-read pastoral leader whose practical experience and reflections are unmatched by any of the academic people mentioned above? And what about the individual Christian who encounters specific problems in an immediate way, more immediate indeed than many of the so-called experts, including the pastoral leader?

It seems clear that one cannot simply restrict the right of theological dissent to the professional theologian. Few theological problems are purely theological. There are often sociological, historical, philosophical, pastoral, and human dimensions which transcend the strictly theological. (Note, for example, the varied composition of the papal birth control commission.)

Everyone in the Church has not only the right but the responsibility to contribute to the solution of a problem according to the measure of professional or personal competence that he possesses. The bishops' pastoral letter should have allowed for this wider exercise of theological dissent.

In the final analysis, theological dissent must always be responsible. This means, among other things, that it must never exceed the competence of the dissenter.

The problem today may not be that too many people are expressing themselves on contemporary religious issues, but that too many people are exceeding their proper level of professional or personal competence. Too many Catholics, without any measure of perceptible scientific competence (either by way of education, lecturing experience, or scholarly publication which has been subject to the review of one's professional peers), may have carelessly entered the area of theological controversy and generated more confusion that light.

Perhaps there would be far less of a crisis atmosphere in the Church if these particular people held themselves in proper restraint. Catholics ought to be less troubled by a careful statement of a professional theologian (or sociologist, or historian, etc.) than by a thunderous scattergun tirade from a pulpit or ominous and largely irresponsible charges and predictions transmitted through conversation and discussion.

Many people in the Church, it now appears, have come to realize that the seminary, college, and catechism theology of the first half of this century was seriously deficient, and they are now in the process of making up for lost time. Their energy and good will are genuinely inspiring.

But there is a similarly large body of Catholics, priests as well as laity, who are reluctant to accept and acknowledge the inadequacies of their own past education and training. Their panic-stricken posture betrays the fact that they have seen, however dimly, that history does not seem to be on their side.

5. *The Meaning and Scope of Magisterium*

I have been arguing throughout this book that the distinctive feature of Catholicism is its conviction that the college of bishops, with the pope at its center and head, is an indispensable factor in the formulation and proclamation of the Gospel of Jesus Christ. For Catholics, the bishops and the pope matter.

While all Christians agree on the importance of Sacred Scripture, for example, they do not agree on the meaning and value of postbiblical Tradition, i.e., Catholics and Protestants do not share the same views on the question of doctrine and dogma.

However, this emphasis on the episcopacy and the papacy, and on doctrine and dogma, has its liabilities. There is a twofold danger: (1) Some Catholics may be led to believe that the formulation and proclamation of doctrine is in the hands of the college of bishops alone, that the Magisterium, in other words, refers only to the pope and the bishops, but that it extends no further. (2) Some may also conclude that that the main task of the teaching authority of the Church is strictly intellectual, i.e., a matter of fashioning abstract statements of faith in precise and technical language.

It would be wrong to study this second chapter of *Dei Verbum* in isolation from other important conciliar documents, especially *Lumen Gentium* (the Dogmatic Constitution on the Church). While *Dei Verbum,* in addressing itself to the problem of doctrinal formulation and proclamation, speaks only of those who succeed in the apostolic office, by episcopal ordination, *Lumen Gentium* (particulary in its second and fourth chapter) speaks of the whole Church as sharing in the prophetic, priestly, and kingly roles of Christ.

This does not mean that the laity can teach, preach, worship, and engage in the secular mission in complete independence of the ordained leadership of the Church. But neither does it mean that the laity simply participate in the *hierarchy's* mission, and then only to the extent that the hierarchy wishes to accommodate them. On the contrary, the Constitution on the Church says that "the lay apostolate . . . is a participation in the saving mission of the Church itself" (art. 33).

Because all members of the Church have been called by baptism to belong to the People of God, there can be no inequality of dignity or of mission. The Church is not a clericalist preserve. Authority resides in the whole community, although its *exercise*, for the sake of the Church's mission, is diversified. The principal, normative expression of the Church's teaching authority occurs in the college of bishops, but this is not the only source or instrument of such authority.

This statement of the Jesuit theological faculty of Alma College, in Los Gatos, California, is difficult to improve upon: "The Church is a community of believers united by the Holy Spirit, who prolongs God's self-revelation in Christ, and does so through men. The work of teaching that this implies goes on in the Church in a hundred different ways: in example and in art, in the words of parents to their children, in sermons and catechesis, in conversation and discussions, lectures and books, in pastoral letters and the declarations of popes and councils. The vivifying presence of the Holy Spirit so guides and protects this total process that the Church as a whole cannot fail in its acceptance and proclamation of God's word. The Church as a whole is infallible" (*America* magazine, September 7, 1968).

In view of the preceding discussion, I would offer these tentative conclusions:

(1) Catholicism is, indeed, distinguished by the importance it ascribes to the Church's college of bishops, and to the pope as the college's principal member. In the formulation and proclamation of the Gospel of Jesus Christ, these official leaders play an indispensable role that cannot be duplicated by any other segment or individual member of the Church.

(2) Nevertheless, the function they perform, while distinctive, is not exclusive. The teaching authority of the Church extends ultimately to the whole Christian community.

(3) The process of communicating and handing on the faith is complex and diverse. The unity of the Church and the fruitfulness of this teaching mission is assured interiorly by the presence of the Holy Spirit, and exteriorly by the presence of the college of bishops within the Church, and by the pope as the principle of unity within the college.

6. What Does the Magisterium Teach?

The whole Church is a teaching community. Every baptized member has a mission to announce the Kingdom of God, and to proclaim the Gospel by word and by example. Magisterium, or teaching authority, resides in the entire Body of Christ, but the *exercise* of this teaching authority varies from individual to individual and from group to group within the Church.

Not all members of the Church are *authentic* teachers. I am not implying, however, that those who

132

are not authentic teachers are hypocrites or false prophets. The word "authentic" is a technical theological term. It indicates that a particular teaching has special authority because of the *office* held by those issuing the pronouncement.

Thus, when the college of bishops takes a stand on some question of faith and morals, a Catholic must consider not only the intrinsic merit of the teaching (i.e., whether or not it makes sense, or reflects the spirit of the Gospel) but also the source from which it comes. The Catholic gives antecedent respect and attention to such doctrinal and moral utterances, not only because of their inner logic, but also because of the official status of those who propose these statements.

This is not to say, however, that every authentic teaching is *accurate* teaching. I am not suggesting that the Catholic looks only to the authority of the teacher and not at all to the intrinsic force of what is being proposed. The Church has never claimed infallibility for all of its doctrinal pronouncements. On the contrary, the First Vatican Council circumscribed very carefully those conditions under which a teaching of the authentic Magisterium might be regarded as free from error.

Since the opposite of infallible is fallible, this means that all noninfallible statements of the Church's teaching authority are subject to error. But a Catholic should not think that the college of bishops will be wrong on about as many occasions as it is right. Ordinarily, he has a right to expect that the various doctrinal and moral guidelines and directives will be substantially accurate, and therefore of some real value in the fulfillment of his mission in the world.

I have suggested above that it would be a mistake to identify the teaching mission of the Church with the hierarchy alone. Now it is time to suggest also that the content of this teaching—whether from the college of bishops, the pope, and/or any other segment of the Church—is not limited to abstract formulations of Christian faith, couched in precise and technical theological language.

The Magisterium, in other words, does not exist merely to settle doctrinal disputes or to condemn theological opinions which seem to conflict with the "tradition of the Church"—no more than the authentic teaching authority of the Church is limited to infallible statements. If this were the case, the Church would have very little to say about very few things. It would have to be, for all practical purposes, completely silent on all the major social and political issues of the day—unless clear-cut doctrinal and moral issues were at stake.

The teaching ministry of the Church is not exhausted by its concern to keep safe and intact the so-called "deposit of faith." Nor is "teaching" limited to verbal or written statements. The Magisterium does not exist simply to issue quasi-legal decrees which indicate to the rest of the Church what they must believe (or not believe) and what they must do (or not do) if they are to be faithful to the original teaching of Christ and therefore if they are to merit eternal salvation.

One cannot easily deny, however, that this has been a common assumption among Catholics. One reason for this may be the emphasis which the Council of Trent (and later the First Vatican Council) placed on the intellectual and static aspects of Christian revelation. Both councils wanted to protect the *objective* character and content of the Gospel: Trent against the Protestants, and Vatican I against the Rationalists and the Fideists. How Vatican II initiated a change in this perspective I have already discussed in the preceding chapter.

7. Interpreting Conciliar Statements

For many years Christians of all denominations resisted the attempts of scholars to study the Bible critically, and Catholics were often more restrained and cautious than most.

It was not until 1943, with the publication of Pope Pius XII's encyclical letter, *Divino Afflante Spiritu,* that Catholic biblical scholars were given the charter to press ahead with a critical interpretation of Sacred Scripture, i.e., to use all available resources (archeological, philological, historical, etc.) in determining the real and literal meaning of the Bible.

The 1964 statement of the Pontifical Biblical Commission on the historicity of the Gospels reinforced this critical trend, and the Dogmatic Constitution on Divine Revelation (see especially Chapter III) provided the strongest official endorsement yet accorded the work of biblical criticism.

This same document insists on the superiority of the Bible over every other expression of faith (see Chaper VI). Therefore, if we can be critical of Sacred Scripture, we can also be critical of something less than Sacred Scripture, namely the official statements of the Church. If fundamentalism is unacceptable in our study of the Bible, so, too, is it unacceptable in our study of Church documents, including those of the Second Vatican Council.

The critical approach asks questions in order to achieve a better understanding: What was the situation at the time of the document's production? What is the meaning of its key terms? Why was this particular plan and style selected? And so forth.

The second chapter of the Dogmatic Constitution on Divine Revelation speaks of the Magisterium as an essential element in our quest of theological understanding. And yet there are many Christians today voicing the opinion that the college of bishops and even the pope himself are obstacles rather than aids to such understanding.

136

If this is true, does it render this second chapter of the Constitution on Divine Revelation meaningless and irrelevant? Not necessarily.

In other words, one must adopt a basically critical attitude toward this particular chapter as toward any text coming forth from the official Church. Why is this so? Because no statement of faith (whether a dogma, a doctrine, or a theological opinion) can ever be regarded as absolutely final and perfect, as if there could be no further development of understanding leading even to a reassessment of the earlier pronouncement.

Furthermore, the Church itself is still on pilgrimage through history. The Christian community stands somewhere "between-the-times": between the Resurrection and the Second Coming of the Lord, between the definitive inbreaking of the Kingdom through Jesus Christ and the final perfection of the Kingdom at the end of history. Every one of its statements, therefore, is always conditioned by this tension between that which has already been fulfilled and that which is yet to be given.

When the Church speaks from the point of view of the promised future (the full realization of the Kingdom in all its glory), she tends to speak in absolutes, as if what has been promised has already been given. Thus, the Church *is* the Body of Christ; the Church *is* one, holy, catholic, and apostolic; and so forth.

When the Church speaks from the point of view of the present (the Kingdom is inaugurated but not fully realized), she tends to speak with greater restraint. Thus, the Church *must become* more fully the Body of Christ; the Church *must become* one, holy, catholic, and apostolic; and so forth.

In the council documents we have a mixture of statements of achievement and statements of principle. The one reminds us of what God has already accomplished in the Church through his saving grace, the other challenges us to live up to the standards God has set for us and the promises he has made.

To a large extent, the statements of *Dei Verbum* (and also of *Lumen Gentium*) on the magisterium are as much statements of principle (i.e., in the realm of yet-to-be-fulfilled promises) as statements of achievement. Apostolicity is· unfinished business.

DISCUSSION QUESTIONS

1. Do you think that the pope and many of the bishops have been too pessimistic about new theological developments, or not pessimistic enough? Why?
2. Did you ever really ask yourself the question, "If we derive our understanding of revelation from the pope and the bishops, where do they derive *their* understanding from?" Do you think that many Catholics, especially those of your

own acquaintance, realize that the pope and the bishops have to learn as well as teach? If not, why do you think this is the case?

3. Do you agree that some Catholics are inconsistent in their attitudes toward the teaching magisterium; namely, that they reject the papal and episcopal teaching on matters of social justice, for example, while embracing such teaching on abortion and birth control? Why do you think this is so? How can this problem be resolved?

4. In the last few years, especially since the publication of the papal encyclical on birth control, Catholic theologians have publicly opposed acclesiastical teachings that were once regarded as fixed and immutable. Does such theological dissent disturb you, encourage you, or not interest you at all? Why?

5. Do you think that lay people have any responsibility at all for the teaching mission of the Church? How can such responsibility be exercised? Do you think that there are adequate outlets and structures for the exercise of this mission right now? If so, indicate what they are. If not, what can and should be done?

6. Do you think that it would make any difference to your Christian faith and witness if suddenly the pope and all the bishops disappeared, never to return? What value do the papacy and the

episcopacy have for the fulfillment of the Church's mission?

7. Do you think the documents of the Second Vatican Council can settle any argument? Are you aware of differences in theological approach in the council documents? Isn't there a danger of picking-and-choosing among the various concilar texts to support our position and undermine another's? How do we overcome this problem?

8. Which documents of the Second Vatican Council have you read in their entirety? Which have you read in part? Whether you have read the documents or not, what is your present impression regarding the relative importance of the various conciliar texts? Which documents do you think are the most important, and why?

6
The Problem of the Papacy

1. Infallibility

It is always a matter of some interest when an individual person or group of people claim to be infallible. This is hardly an ordinary posture for those who prize intelligence and reason and who are, at the same time, conscious of their deficiencies and limitations. And yet toward the end of the last century, at the First Vatican Council, the Catholic Church made such a claim for itself and for its principal leader, the pope.

Of course, every Catholic should know that infallibility was intended to mean only freedom from doctrinal error, not access to all truth, and that it could only be engaged under certain strict conditions: (1) the matter to be proposed must pertain directly to the Gospel ("faith and morals"); (2) it is proposed for the belief of the whole Church; and, in the case of the pope, (3) it is proposed *ex cathedra* (literally: "from the chair"), i.e., when the pope is "acting in the office of shepherd and teacher of all Christians . . . by virtue of his supreme apostolic authority."

With regard to the pope, the council suggested that his infallibility is the same infallibility "with which the divine Redeemer willed his Church to be endowed." It is the Church as a community which has been given the Spirit of truth and which cannot fundamentally err in its understanding of the heart of the Gospel. The pope is infallible only insofar as he enunciates and proclaims the infallible faith of the whole Church, Catholic and non-Catholic. He is not infallible unto himself, in complete independence from the Church.

But the authors of our catechisms, college religion textbooks, and seminary manuals extended infallibility to unilateral papal statements regarding matters which do not directly pertain to the Gospel, to pronouncements which could not possibly commend themselves to the belief of the whole Church, and to declarations of the pope even when he did not solemnly and explicitly engage his office as chief shepherd and teacher.

Thus, in the wake of the First Vatican Council (which ended before it had a chance to take up the question of the episcopacy, thereby leaving the impression that the pope is the only voice that really counts in the Church), some theologians began extending the possibilities of infallibility to every newsworthy utterance of the Bishop of Rome, whether in papal encyclicals, Christmas and Easter messages, special communications to the Roman Curia, or personal addresses to particular groups (e.g., midwives, jurists, etc.).

The first half of this century has been a time of exaggerated papal authority, with the insistence on infallibility more a defense of centralized authority than an issue of practical import. (After all, infallibility was employed but once since its definition at Vatican I). Bishops were regarded by some as the mere vicars or delegates of the pope, serving at his pleasure. Their task and the function of other office-holders in the Church was supposedly one of explanation, defense, dissemination, and implementation of papal views and directives.

Indeed, the acceptable theologian was not the one who could critically examine the data of revelation in the quest for a better understanding of the Gospel. That type was often constrained and censured (M-J. Lagrange, Yves Congar, L. Charlier, H. deLubac, K. Rahner, John Courtney Murray, *et al.*). Official favor was reserved for those schooled in "orthodoxy," those who faithfully explained and defended papal statements, past and present, and who could find support for the conclusions of these statements in Scripture, the Fathers, St. Thomas, and earlier documents of the Church.

These were the people who, logically enough, opposed the doctrine of collegiality at the Second Vatican Council. Some of them even called the idea heretical. For if the pope is the one supreme and absolute teacher in the Church, why should he have to refer himself to the bishops? In fact, why should there be any further need for ecumenical councils?

But Pope John XXIII, much to the consternation of this group, called a council and that council rejected the narrow papalist theology that had dominated early 20th-century Catholicism. The pope is the head of the college of bishops, to be sure, but he is nothing without the college. The college, too, is nothing without the pope, but it is grossly misleading to call his authority "supreme and absolute." Only God himself has claim to that.

Consequently, there can be no theological foundation for the common view that, "for all practical purposes," Catholics must give the same response to non-infallible papal statements as they would give to solemnly promulgated dogmatic definitions of the Church. But that is what was being urged in the recent debate about *Humanae Vitae*. "For all practical purposes," it was argued, the Catholic's response to an encyclical must be the same as his response to the Gospel of St. Luke, the Epistle to the Romans, or the decrees of the Council of Chalcedon.

Too many Catholics believe that "practical infallibility" is binding upon them. It is not. It is a theological fiction which can neither be supported nor sustained. Happily, the present debate about infallibility has seen to it that its days are numbered, and so too may be the lifespan of the narrow theology that has supported it until now.

2. *Apostolic Succession*

I should guess that, in the minds of many Catholics, "apostolic succession" means that the bishops possess the full authority of the original apostles because they can trace their episcopal orders back, in an uninterrupted sequence of the laying on of hands, to the time of Christ and the Twelve. Theologians are now referring to this particular concept as "mechanical" and are suggesting that such a notion needs rethinking in the light of the ecumenical movement and the renewal of biblical studies. [See, for example, *Apostolic Succession,* ed. H. Küng (Concilium, vol. 34), Paulist Press, 1968].

The substance of the traditional Catholic understanding of apostolic succession is contained in article 20 of the council's Dogmatic Constitution on the Church. The document insists that the divine mission, entrusted by Christ to the apostles, must last until the end of the world (Mt. 28:20), and "for this reason the apostles took care to appoint successors in this hierarchically structured society."

And just as the apostles had gathered others around them to assist in fulfilling the mission of the Church, so do we now have a variety of ministries within the Church today. "Among those various ministries . . . the chief place belongs to the office of those who, appointed to the episcopate in a sequence running back to the beginning, are the ones who pass on the apostolic seed." It is through the bishops, therefore, that the apostolic tradition is manifested and preserved throughout the world.

All other ministries within the Church (especially the priesthood and the diaconate) are to be united with the episcopate in the service of the community: in the teaching of doctrine, in sacred worship, and in the maintenance of good order. The ministry of the episcopate is permanent because the needs of the community are permanent.

Catholic theology is not about to abandon the notion of apostolic succession. The Church will always be institutionalized and structured, and the episcopate will always be a part of that framework— even though its form and style may change almost beyond recognition.

But there is a larger, more positive sense in which we are to understand "apostolic succession." It must refer primarily to the *whole* Church. It means that the Church as such, in its witness and in its mission, is faithful to the witness and mission of the original apostles. The whole Church can lay claim to apostolic succession, and to the extent that its ministry to the poor, the hungry, the destitute, and the alienated is the same as the apostolic ministry to mankind.

Strictly speaking, the apostolic office cannot be transmitted beyond the apostolic period itself. Only the apostles were firsthand witnesses of the Resurrection (Acts 4:33), and only they received the direct mandate from Christ himself (Mk. 16:15; Mt. 28:18-

20; Lk. 10:16). But the task which they received remains unfinished: the Church must witness to the Lordship of Jesus through all generations and it must carry on his ministry of love and service to all mankind, in every land and in every age of history.

Apostolic succession applies, in the first instance, to the whole Church, and then to the body of bishops within the Church. For the whole Church is the new people of God; the whole Church is the temple of the Holy Spirit; the whole Church is the Body of Christ and the sign and instrument of God's Kingdom.

It is the Catholic conviction, nonetheless, that the Church cannot remain faithful to the apostolic witness and mission without the assistance and direction of proper leadership. Overseers *(episcopoi)* have been given to the Christian community to help and inspire the Church to remain faithful to its apostolic foundation, to confess without equivocation the Lordship of Jesus and to pursue without compromise his quest for the Kingdom of God.

It is always difficult for the Church to maintain a proper balance between the apostolic succession as it applies to the whole Church and the apostolic succession as it applies more narrowly to the college of bishops within the Church. The fidelity of the Church to the apostolic witness and mission must somehow grow out of the dialectical tension between these two realities. At times the strain of that tension seems disruptive of the Church's unity, as in the present situation. But it is also the Catholic's conviction that the healing Spirit will preserve her life and insure her apostolic faithfulness.

I should expect, therefore, that the average Catholic's understanding of apostolic succession will undergo the same modification as his prior understanding of sacramental causality.

There was a time when we so emphasized the sacraments as "causes of grace" that some forgot that the sacraments cannot cause grace unless they are, in the first instance, "signs of faith." Infant baptism was proposed as the ordinary rather than as the extraordinary celebration of a sacrament, for it supposedly demonstrated as no other sacrament could that all the sacraments cause grace automatically, so long as the recipient places no obstacles in the way (i.e., mortal sin or denial of faith). We presumed this to be the "traditional" view until theological scholarship undermined it.

Liturgical scholars deserve much of the credit for redirecting our attention to the marvelous balance of sign and cause in the genuinely traditional theology of St. Thomas Aquinas (see Godfrey Diekmann, O.S.B., *Come, Let Us Worship*, Doubleday Image Book: 1966, pp. 35-51). Part III of the *Summa* became a primary source in the contemporary renewal of Catholic worship and sacramental theology. Edward Schillebeeckx's *Christ the Sacrament of Encounter* is a good example of the present day influence of Aquinas.

But the reaction against the Protestant Reformation has left its mark on the Catholic consciousness, and it is deeper than most of us would care to admit. For a long time we resisted the notion of "priesthood of the faithful" because it seemed to be linked with the rejection of Holy Order. We were wary of placing too much stress on the Bible, because it seemed to imply a de-emphasis on the teaching authority of the Church. We were insistent upon the almost automatic communication of grace in a sacrament, because we did not want to identify ourselves with the Protestant emphasis on "faith alone."

Even today, many Catholics become very nervous about appeals to the primacy of conscience, because this seems to reduce the Christian faith to private interpretation and a totally subjective morality.

So, too, the idea that apostolic succession applies primarily to the whole Church and only secondarily to the bishops within the Church will be resisted for its "Protestant" overtones. But the same theological issues that were at stake in the case of the sacraments are at stake here.

The mere fact that a group of men, called "bishops," can trace its ordination back to the first century is no guarantee, in itself, that the Church which they serve is faithful to the apostolic tradition and is thereby superior to every other religious community in the world.

149

What good is accomplished, for example, if the Eucharist is celebrated "validly" by a group of bigots who do not know the meaning of brotherly love? Is their Eucharist automatically superior to the religious services of those who are struggling for God's Kingdom but who do not accept the Tridentine doctrine of transubstantiation? Can one responsibly suggest that the Eucharistic mystery is fully present where valid orders and valid doctrine exist, and entirely absent where such validity does not exist, even though the love of Christ is there?

By the same token, no Church, and certainly not the Catholic Church, can take ultimate pride in the fact that its college of bishops is in the right historical line back to the time of Christ and the apostles. For this is only one aspect of the problem. Historical continuity merely highlights the apostolic responsibility that devolves upon those who claim it.

The apostolic succession of the bishops is not "valid" simply because historical research can demonstrate certain links throughout history (as if it were a kind of clerical relay-race). Their apostolic succession is credible only because they and the community which they serve are faithful to the witness and ministry of the apostles. To the extent that the bishops or the community are not faithful to this tradition, to that same extent is the question of "validity" an irrelevant one.

Article 21 of the Dogmatic Constitution on the Church reminds us that it is Christ alone who guarantees the effectiveness of every act of the Church. He alone is the "supreme High Priest." It is Christ who gives fruitfulness to the preaching of the Word and the celebration of the sacraments. But not automatically, by way of a kind of religious magic. He must be accepted in faith, and only in faith does he have the power to reach men.

Catholics are not about to yield their conviction that the college of bishops, with the pope at its center and head, is necessary to the witness and ministry of the Church. But they can no longer be interested simply in making it a matter of historical research into an unbroken series of valid ordinations. The area of concern is shifting from these "mechanical" considerations to the paramount concern that, in this community and in this college of bishops, the commitment to the apostolic witness and ministry is unmistakably clear.

3. Collegiality

Before the Second Vatican Council, Catholics often assumed that the Church was an essentially monarchical institution. Although religious authority was also exercised by bishops and priests, such authority was simply derived from that of the one supreme leader of the Church, namely the pope. When all was said and done, it was the pope—and the pope alone

—who ran the Church. And this was the way Christ wanted it—or so it was thought.

Article 22 of the Dogmatic Constitution on the Church proposes a view which challenges most Catholics to change their understanding of the basic structure of the Church. It can no longer be regarded as a monarchical institution, with all authority residing ultimately in the person of the pope.

Lumen Gentium teaches that a college of bishops exists within the Church, and that every bishop has power insofar as he is a member of this college. The bishop is not, as some Catholics seemed to think, merely the vicar or delegate of the pope.

The college of bishops continues the college of the apostles, but one cannot argue that the two colleges are the same in every respect. However, the council implies that just as the college of the apostles existed by the decree of the Lord, so does the college of bishops. In other words, we could not really conceive of the Church existing without some form of episcopal ministry.

True to its abiding concern to protect the primacy of the pope, the council reminds us that this college of bishops exists only insofar as it takes in the pope as its head. Without the pope, there is no college. But this does not mean that the pope is the sole principle of unity in the college. Unity is also insured by the presence of the Holy Spirit, fraternal love, common faith, and various other manifestations of the *communion.* We know, for example, that the Church retains its unity even during the period between the death of one pope and the election of another.

Furthermore, the college of bishops is the possessor of supreme and full authority over the whole Church (see the Code of Canon Law, c. 228, n. 1). This authority, although never independent of the pope, is not bestowed upon the college by the pope.

The pope and the other bishops are members of the same college. There are not two centers of supreme and full authority, but only one, i.e., the college of bishops with the pope at the center and head. (The pope's personal proposal to the Theological Commission in 1964 was rejected; namely, that the pope should be regarded as "answerable to the Lord alone in his action." The council insisted, against the pope, that the successor of Peter is bound to the revelation of God, the fundamental structure of the Church, the sacraments, definitions of earlier councils, and other obligations far too numerous to list.)

Although the text of article 22 represents a major advance over the theology of the First Vatican Council, there remains an exaggerated concern for the primacy of the pope. Whereas the council correctly insisted that the college is nothing without the pope, it did not emphasize that the pope is nothing without the college. And yet this must follow if, in fact, the college possesses supreme and full authority in the Church. There cannot be two independent centers of such authority in one and the same organization. There can only be one center; namely, the college of bishops with the pope at the head. The college is nothing without the pope, and the pope is nothing without the college.

Out of context, however, there are many statements in the council documents—and particularly here in the 22nd article of *Lumen Gentium*—which seem to be saying what many Catholics have always felt: the pope is really the only voice that ultimately matters. It's nice if he can work with the body of bishops and come to some common conclusions through healthy dialogue and collaboration. But this is really superfluous. In the final analysis, what the pope says goes, regardless of the convictions and sentiments of the rest of the Church.

There is too much emphasis here, as well, on the legal rights of the pope and the bishops, and not nearly enough about their moral obligations as pastors and servants of the Church. Structural self-justification has been an understandable preoccupation of the Catholic Church, particularly since the challenge of the Protestant Reformation. But the historical and theological situation has changed markedly. The approach of *Lumen Gentium* now appears unnecessarily defensive and one-sided.

4. Uniformity vs. Pluriformity

A single sentence, nestled obscurely in some ecclesiastical document, can become the source of a
major theological, pastoral, or spiritual development
within the Church. One thinks immediately of that
key statement in Vatican II's Pastoral Constitution
on the Church in the Modern World: "Thus, the
human race has passed from a rather static concept
of reality to a more dynamic, evolutionary one" (art.
5, para. 4).

Article 23 of *Lumen Gentium*, despite its highly
predictable language about the pope as "the Roman
Pontiff, the successor of Peter, . . . the perpetual and
visible source and foundation of the unity of the
bishops and of the multitude of the faithful," suggests
that the real pluriformity existing even within the
Roman Catholic Church can be attributed to the
workings of divine Providence.

The sentence reads: "By divine Providence it has
come about that various churches established in diverse places by the apostles and their successors have
in the course of time coalesced into several groups,
organically united, which, preserving the unity of
faith and the unique divine constitution of the universal Church, enjoy their own discipline, their own
liturgical usage, and their own theological and spiritual heritage" (art. 23, para. 5).

When Catholics ask what the Church will be like
in the post-ecumenical era, many cling to the belief

that it will be the same sociologically recognizable religious community. The numbers will be increased. Many of "those others" will be among us, acknowedging the supremacy and infallibility of the pope, duly celebrating and receiving all seven sacraments, and rendering proper homage to the blessed Mother of God. There will be uniformity of discipline, uniformity of worship, uniformity of theology, and uniformity of spirituality. The age of confusion will be over. All Catholics will be operating again on the same general wave length. Religion will become, once more, a recognizable enterprise.

Such a position is wrong on several levels, particularly the sociological and the theological. Those who continue to believe that the Catholic Church is passing through a mere phase in its history, that all will return to "normal" (i.e., the sociological situation of the first half of this century) betray an uncritical understanding of what is going on in the world today. But, then, our tradition has never been strong on empirical investigation, objective analysis, and careful projection, of the sort attempted, for example, in the remarkable volume, *The Year 2000: A Framework for Speculation on the Next Thirty-three Years* (edited by Herman Kahn and A. J. Wiener), New York: Macmillan, 1967.

The belief in the return to "stability" is wrong on theological grounds as well. It assumes that unity demands uniformity. And yet uniformity has never been an accepted goal of Church life at any significant moment in its history, and certainly not in the New Testament beginnings. The Church has always encouraged and embraced a variety of liturgical rites, a diversity of disciplinary arrangements, a pluralism of theologies, and a pluriformity of spiritualties.

Vatican II reminds us there, in a chapter which is otherwise so thoroughly committed to the distinctively Roman and Western concept of ecclesiastical order, that pluriformity in worship, discipline, theology, and spirituality is a gift of divine Providence.

While the Council is speaking here of the various Eastern "uniate" communities within the Roman Catholic Church, the theological principle applies as well to the whole body of Christian churches: Orthodox, Anglican, and Protestant. We need not attempt to cover over the real differences that separate one from the other. But in our common quest for unity, we must come to realize that a spirit of flexibility and tolerance of legitimate differences and emphases is to be encouraged.

The Church of the post-ecumenical era (whenever that might be) will, in all likelihood, not be recognizable by early 20th-century Catholic standards. It will be a Church of newly won unity in the Holy Spirit but with more, not less, pluriformity of liturgy, discipline, theology, and spirituality. Catholic liturgists know this; Catholic canon lawyers, historians and sociologists know this; Catholic theologians

157

know this; and many Catholic pastoral leaders know this. But the present crisis in the Church indicates that the acceptance of such pluriformity will not come easily.

Besides a renewed concern for empirical analysis, objective self-criticism, and genuine theological scholarship, the Church will need a good dose of patience and compassion for those (including many ecclesiastical officeholders) who do not yet share this perspective.

5. *Authority in the Church*

Dr. Robert McAfee Brown, Professor of Religion at Stanford University, has always enjoyed a good reputation among Catholics, even among those whose support of the ecumenical movement has not been marked by fervor and enthusiasm. Dr. Brown is a safely predictable Protestant, just as Mr. Roy Wilkins, of NAACP, is a safely predictable Negro. Both are moderate, reasonable, and essentially optimistic men. Both have had a reassuring effect on the "natural enemies" of their own group.

In an article in *Commonweal* (September 6, 1968), Dr. Brown presumes upon the trust and respect most knowledgeable Catholics have in him and for him. The encyclical of Pope VI on the regulation of births, Dr. Brown suggests, is "inadvertently the greatest gift to the ecumenical scene since the election of Pope John back in 1959. For its reception shows conclusively that traditional views of papal authority simply cannot be taken seriously any more, and that Catholics feel no greater sense of being bound to unquestionable doctrine than do Protestants."

He asks us to consider the alternatives. Suppose that the pope had left the question to the individual consciences of married people. Such a position would have been eminently credible and the teaching authority of the pope would have been enhanced rather than diminished. The ecumenical movement would have remained as "hung up" about the papacy as before.

Had the pope actually changed the earlier teaching in the light of recent studies, the non-Catholic Christian certainly "would have been forced to develop a new theology about an authoritative teaching office focussed in one man as a viable pattern for the ecclesiastical future, and the resultant groanings and travail within Protestantism would have been divisive to the uttermost."

But the pope pursued neither course. Instead he reaffirmed without qualification the teaching of *Casti Connubii* banning all methods of birth control with the exception of rhythm and abstinence. The encyclical, Dr. Brown argues, "is so out of touch . . . that it is impossible to take it seriously as a definitive statement of Catholic teaching, or as one that reflects the kind of claims that have been traditionally associated with the solemn teaching authority of the papal office."

Accordingly, what this encyclical has succeeded in doing is to have raised in a dramatically public manner the more radical question of authority in the Church, and specifically the authority of the pope. Had the position of the encyclical been other than what it was, the question of authority might have been postponed for many more years.

Catholics who, until now, have simply taken the authority of the pope for granted can no longer avoid doing some hard thinking about the matter. The issue is out in the open.

Are the assumptions of early 20th-century theology valid after all? Is the pope the only voice that really counts in the Church? And if his position is not so absolute as we previously imagined, does that mean that authority has vanished from the Church? In other words, does religious authority reside only in the pope and the bishops?

The statement of the 11 Jesuit theologians of Alma College in Los Gatos, Calif., to which I referred earlier, provides a basis on which these questions can be answered: "The Church is a community of believers united by the Holy Spirit, who prolongs God's self-revelation in Christ, and does so through men. The work of teachings that this implies goes on in the Church in a hundred different ways: in example and in art, in words of parents to their children, in

160

sermons and catechesis, in conversation and discussions, lectures and books, in pastoral letters and the declarations of popes and councils.

"The vivifying presence of the Holy Spirit so guides and protects this total process that the Church as a whole cannot fail in its acceptance and proclamation of God's word. The Church as a whole is infallible."

The statement is completely faithful to the central tradition of the Church and of its theology. But as Karl Rahner, S.J., is fond of saying: one cannot hope to understand contemporary theology unless he begins with and thoroughly masters the traditional theology.

What became increasingly clear as the debate about *Humanae Vitae* unfolded was that a great many "traditional" Catholics had not mastered the traditional theology. The task of reeducating both the clergy and the laity became larger than previously supposed. In too many cases, we could no longer presume a traditional base upon which to build.

6. *The Pope and Birth Control*

In one of my weekly newspaper columns written a year before the papal encyclical on birth control, I had suggested that "it is one of the great theological and pastoral tragedies of our time that the average Christian's attitude toward the papacy and papal authority should be formed exclusively within the context of the birth control issue." The publication of *Humanae Vitae* a year later provided an occasion for reaffirming this judgment with an even deeper sense of urgency.

Various opinions within the Church had already become dangerously hardened prior to the encyclical's appearance in July, 1968. Once the pope had chosen to endorse the minority point of view, there developed a tendency on the part of some Catholics to begin reading one another out of the Church or for some to leave the Church on their own initiative, in sadness and disillusionment. (The editor of a right-of-center Catholic magazine called for such an exodus on the left.)

Either course of action would reflect an implicit acceptance of the post-Vatican I ecclesiology which exalted the pope to the status of a supertheologian and clothed his every pronouncement with the aura of impeccable and incontrovertible accuracy.

But the theology that has developed over the past several decades and which emerged so unexpectedly (for many Catholics) at the Second Vatican Council has produced in the Church today a more critical attitude toward papal authority—an attitude which eschews both cynicism and rigidity. It portrays the pope for what he is: the leading moral authority in the Church who, nevertheless, shares our human condition in all things, including sin and error. His authority, though supreme, is never divorced from that of the rest of the college of bishops, nor indeed can it be independent of the Spirit that has been given to the whole Church.

Furthermore, as Archbishop Ferdinando Lambruschini made clear when releasing the document in Rome, this encyclical is not infallible. It is subject, therefore, to error and later correction, and that is why he made it a point to invite theologians and other specialists in the Church to discuss and debate this declaration.

One should not conclude, however, that a Catholic may adopt a casual or indifferent attitude to major pronouncements such as this one. The pope is the chief spokesman for the entire Christian community. He is the heart and center of the college of bishops and, as such, is a symbol of unity for the whole Church. In the formation of one's conscience the Catholic must pay serious heed to the pastoral and theological directives of his Church's principal bishop.

Accordingly, it would be irresponsible for a Catholic to dismiss this encyclical without study, consultation, and prayer. It is not a light matter to adopt a moral position at odds with the pope's. However, those who so decide must be spared the pharisaical abuse that issues such as this so often provoke.

But why should a Catholic respond with some measure of enthusiasm to the call of the pope on issues of war and peace or social justice (where infallibility is similarly not at stake) when this same Catholic may seem cool, if not in open opposition, on other matters, e.g., the 1968 "Credo" of Pope Paul VI or his birth control encyclical? Is there a radical inconsistency here? Have we reverted once again to the pick-and-choose polemics of the 1940's and the 1950's when Catholics would quote fragments of papal statements against one another?

Inconsistency is a problem only for those who uncritically accept the ecclesiology of the early twentieth century: the pope is the one theologian that ultimately matters and what he says goes.

Yet it has become exceedingly awkward today for many Catholics to support this rigid view of papal authority. For example, we have some of them saying that the pope has spoken authoritatively on contraception, but he is "naive" about nuclear disarmament or the Vietnam war. There is to be no compromise or discussion about the clear strictures of his birth control statement (indeed, Catholics who don't like it should leave the Church), but we can imagine all sorts of "factors" to mitigate and effectively nullify the force of his social encyclical, *Populorum Progressio,* or Pope John XXIII's *Mater et Magistra* (we recall the flippancy: "Mater, si; magistra, no!").

The traditionalist must somehow resolve his own special problems. My concern here is for those who may have grown cynical about the papacy, particularly in view of this recent pronouncement, but who may still recognize the call of the Gospel in so many papal utterances and gestures (e.g., his appearance in 1965 before the United Nations). For it is precisely in proclaiming the Gospel that the pope fulfills his role as chief shepherd and holy father. If the proclamation is genuinely evangelical, the Holy Spirit will see to the echo throughout the whole Church; if it is not, he will see to the static.

On the birth control issue the pope's present position may not seem to reflect the consensus of the Church, and static fills the air. The encyclical is at odds with the conclusions of the overwhelming majority of the pope's own commission of experts, the public resolutions of the Third World Lay Congress in Rome, a large number of Catholic moral theologians, the consciences of many Catholic married couples, and the pastoral and theological judgments of the large majority of non-Catholic Christian churches which participate in the life of the Body of Christ and in his Spirit.

If the teaching of *Humanae Vitae* is faithful to the authentic tradition of the Gospel, it will eventually produce a consensus of approval throughout the whole Church. If not, it will take its place with past authoritative statements on religious liberty, interest-taking, the salvation of non-Catholics, and the ends of marriage. Many expect that this will happen.

Meanwhile the debate enters yet another major phase with this important ingredient. Confusion will be compounded if this interim period is not marked by clarity of argument and charity of manner. Ridicule and recrimination, flippancies and fulminations will only serve to compromise the Church's enduring mission to be the sign and special instrument of God's Kingdom on earth and the community of hope for the future of mankind. This is hardly the time for closing doors, particularly in one another's faces.

7. *"The Credo of the People of God"*

Pope Paul VI concluded the Year of Faith with a new "Credo of the People of God." This profession of faith was not really a creed in the classic sense, as, for example, the one proposed by the Council of Nicaea in the year 325 and which we recite in substance every Sunday at Mass.

What we have here in this papal statement is a mixture of universally binding and universally accepted doctrines, on the one hand, and some thoroughly arguable theological opinions, on the other. The intrusion of this latter material has assured the new "Credo" the status of a controversial document. Indeed, the pope and his personal theological advisers must have expected the criticism which the profession of faith encountered.

The pope insisted in his introductory remarks that his profession of faith "repeats in substance, with some developments called for by the spiritual condition of our time, the creed of Nicaea," to which I referred above. Had his theological consultants followed this plan more closely, the "Credo" could have more easily achieved the purpose for which it was written: to strengthen every Catholic's "desire to live by (the Gospel) in the historical circumstances in which the Church finds herself in her pilgrimage in the midst of the world."

Instead, in far too many instances, the writers of the "Credo" seemed to have engaged in theological polemics in the apparent hope of using the vast authority and influence of the papacy to embarrass or to suppress theological views at odds with their own. This was an objectionable tactic when it was employed by the theologians who assisted Pope Pius XII in writing *Humani Generis* in 1950, and it is no less objectionable here.

Despite some careless talk to the contrary, most Catholics still regard the pope as the chief spokesman for the Body of Christ, the one to whom we look as a symbol of unity and the pattern of Christian life for all the faithful. The fact that this new "Credo" soon became a bone of contention and the occasion of some strong words, bordering at times on the cynical, indicates that the papal theologians in this case may have done the pope and his office a distinct disservice.

Any statement which offers itself as a summation of contemporary Catholic belief should, as far as possible, reflect the actual consensus of that belief. It should never exalt one theological point of view over another in matters which are still open to legitimate debate. A few examples (taken in the order in which they appear in the document) will suffice to show that such care was not taken here.

(1) Some Catholics, for what reason I do not know, have made something of an issue of the existence or non-existence of angels. The "Credo" dignifies this debate by making a special point of the existence of angels in the very first paragraph (alongside our most fundamental belief in God), even though the classic creeds of Nicaea and Constantinople do not mention them.

(2) Some Catholics have been disturbed by the vernacular translations of the Mass and have even suggested that the liturgy is teaching heresy when it speaks of Jesus' being raised from the dead by the Father rather than by his own power. The "Credo" insists that Jesus rose "of his own power" and makes no mention at all of the consistent teaching of the New Testament that "God has raised him up" (Acts 2:24).

(3) Catholics have never been happy about the thought of Hell, but some Catholics are apparently more unhappy about the possibility that it doesn't exist at all (at least in the way that we have pictured it in the past). So the "Credo" reminds us that those who reject the Gospel will go "to the fire that is not extinguished."

(4) Most Catholics know there is some controversy about original sin today, and even though the issues in the debate are too technical for them, they are not comfortable with differences of opinion on a matter they thought was settled centuries ago. The "Credo" endorses the view of one theological school which continues to insist (as is their academic right) that original sin is a personal offense committed by a particular individual named Adam, and, furthermore, that our "first parents" enjoyed special, superhuman gifts which we would have inherited had it not been for their moral folly.

(5) There are Catholics today, including priests, who have begun to wonder about the propriety of baptizing infants. Shouldn't the decision to embrace the Gospel and join the Church be a mature and deliberate one, to be made only by one who has the intellectual and psychological capacity to do so? There are, in fact, some good theological reasons for the acceptance of infant baptism, but not the one given in the "Credo": that children are "born deprived of supernatural grace." The "Credo" thereby takes a stand on the nature-and-grace discussion which is hardly near maturity and it implicitly endorses the earlier belief in Limbo. At least the document supports the theological basis (absence of grace in newly-born children) for this idea.

(6) Many Catholics are troubled with the new style of celebrating Mass and with all the talk about

community worship and the common meal. The "Credo" emphasizes only the sacrificial nature of the Mass and speaks of the ordained priest as offering the sacrifice "in the name of" the Church. The Second Vatican Council's Constitution on the Sacred Liturgy is not mentioned and its liturgical theology and pastoral orientation is absent.

(7) Transubstantiation is presented, for all practical purposes, as the only orthodox manner of explaining the Real Presence of Christ in the Eucharist, even though this is still a matter of some discussion in Catholic theology (not that theologians are suggesting that Christ is not present in the Eucharist, but that transubstantiation is not the only way, or necessarily the best way, of explaining this presence).

(8) What disturbs some Catholics most about changes in the Church is the deepened appreciation of the social apostolate of the Church. George Gallup discovered recently that 57 per cent of American Roman Catholics reject the involvement of the Church in matters of political and social consequence. The "Credo," therefore, assures us that the Kingdom of God which we seek is in the next world, that insofar as it exists here and now, it consists in knowledge of Christ, hope in eternal blessings, an ardent response to the love of God, and the bestowal grace and holiness among men. The Pastoral Constitution on the Church in the Modern World, where service (*di-*

170

akonia) is portrayed as part of the Church's essential mission, is not mentioned.

At one point, the new "Credo" expresses its agreement with the council that there must be within the Church a "rich variety of liturgical rites and the legitimate diversity of theological and spiritual heritages and special disciplines, (which) far from injuring her unity, make it more manifest."

"The 'Credo' of the People of God," insofar as it repeats and reaffirms the historic faith of Nicaea and Constantinople, provides an occasion for strengthening our desire to live the Gospel and pursue without compromise the contemporary mission of the Church.

But insofar as this document allows the views of one particular school of theology (a minority view, let it be added, that was clearly rejected at Vatican II) to intrude itself upon the ground of authentic Christian tradition, the "Credo" has transformed itself from an expression of common faith binding the whole Church together, into a personal brief on behalf of one party in the current theological debate.

DISCUSSION QUESTIONS

1. What do you mean by "papal infallibility?" If the pope were not infallible after all, what difference would that fact make in the life and mission of the Church?

2. What do you mean by "apostolic succession?" If it were discovered by some historian that papal

or episcopal orders were not validly transmitted at some point in history, would that undermine the claim of the Catholic Church to be the Body of Christ, faithful to the mandate of Christ and his Apostles? If so, why? If not, why not?

3. Do you think that a Catholic can oppose the papal teaching on birth control and still remain a Catholic in good standing? If not, why not? If so, why?

4. Before reading this chapter, did you remember that, in June of 1968, the pope had issued "The Credo of the People of God?" Do you have a copy of this "Credo?" If so, how many times do you refer to it? Why do you think the "Credo" made the impact it did?

7

Bishops and Pastors:

1. Ordained Ministry as Religious Leadership

Political campaigns have been criticized because too often the candidates are marketed like soap products. When the office seeker is judged solely on the basis of personal appearance, popular appeal, television image, and so forth, the people are left with no useful criteria by which to evaluate the candidate's performance in office. Apparently he forfeits his right to reelection when these essentially superficial qualities begin to slip away from him.

Not all candidates and voters are personality-oriented, however. There are issue-oriented office seekers and voters, too. The issue-oriented candidate usually offers a more objective basis for evaluation. The voter can determine whether or not he agrees with the candidate's views on the major issues of the day and then, if the candidate is elected, the voter can study his voting record and the posture he adopts in speeches and administrative action.

Although we have no public campaigns for ecclesiastical office, there is as great a need in the Church for standards of evaluation as there is in government. All of the People of God are responsible for the mission of the Church (Dogmatic Constitution on the Church, n. 30 and 33). This is contrary to the assumption underlying the Catholic Action movement of the 1940's and 1950's when the lay apostolate was conceived as a participation in the mission of the hierarchy.

Since leadership plays such a crucial part in the fulfillment of that mission, the membership of the Church should know what it has a right to expect from its bishops and pastors.

Indeed, if there is anything which is particularly characteristic of recent theological discussion about the priesthood, it is the central thesis that ordination to the priesthood introduces someone to a new responsibility of religious leadership within, and even over against, the Christian community. (This is in contrast with the more traditional view of the priest as a kind of "super-Christian," an *alter Christus,* a man of power, who is closest to God and to Christ and who is thereby in a position to dispense both saving truth and saving grace in word and in sacrament.)

This newer approach is advanced in such articles as Father Edward Schillebeeckx's "Towards a More Adequate Theology of Priesthood" (*Theology Digest,* summer, 1970) and Father Walter Kasper's "A New Dogmatic Outlook on the Priestly Ministry" (*Concilium,* vol. 43, 1969), in the pastoral letter of the American Catholic Bishops ("Statement on Celibacy," November 13, 1969), and in various sections of the council documents, especially the second chapter of the Decree on the Bishops' Pastoral Office in the Church.

According to Schillebeeckx, the ordained Christian must so "guide the Christian life of the community that Christ may really be its only Lord." He must be able "to take the lead in the service of the Word (and) to lead the community's sacramental celebrations."

The pastor is called "to administer the 'consolation of the Scriptures' (Rom. 15:4) by admonition and exhortation (and) to take the lead in the love that seeks justice first of all, i.e., to promote the concern which the community should show for man in his concrete historical situation." This means he must be a man capable of mounting a measured and responsible critique against both society and the Church itself.

Father Kasper develops an understanding of priest as community leader based on an analysis of the New Testament, with special reference to the section on the ministries of service in Rom. 12 and 1 Cor. 12. Every Christian possesses his own charism, or gift of the Spirit, but every charism is meant to serve the common good (1 Cor. 12:7). No one person can possess all the charisms or do everything that is to be done by the Church.

However, there exists a charism of administrative leadership (1 Cor. 12:8) whose function it is to integrate and coordinate all of the other charisms. The charism of administrative leadership thereby serves the unity and mission of the Church (on this point, see also the Dogmatic Constitution on the Church, n. 30).

"To formulate a new understanding of the priestly office," Father Kasper argues, "we must begin with the charism of community leadership."

Similarly, the Catholic bishops of the United States have spoken of the problems and goals of the priesthood in terms of community leadership: "If the Church is for the world, 'the priest is for the Church.' The work of building that Church as the community of persons united in Christ is the task of all her members. Still, Christ has provided his Church with *the special ministry of leadership,* to be exercised in preaching the word, celebrating the mysteries, and forming the Christian community." The bishops refer to this ministry of leadership as the *"distinctive service of priests to the Church and to mankind"* (paras. 5-6, italics mine).

But what does it really mean to speak of the bishop and the priest as exercising a ministry of leadership within and for the Church? How does the Church evaluate the effectiveness of its leaders and how does it decide upon the fitness of those who aspire to the priesthood?

Fortunately, the Second Vatican Council has provided us with a remarkably detailed job description for a bishop, in the second chapter of its Decree on the Bishops' Pastoral Office in the Church. What the council says about the qualifications and responsibilities of a bishop also applies to the office of pastor since a man holding pastoral leadership over a particular eucharistic community (a parish or some other special group) functions, for all practical purposes, as the bishop (literally: "overseer") of that community.

2. The Ordained Ministry and the Ministry of the Whole Church

(A)   If the Church exists to proclaim the coming of the Kingdom of God in Christ, an ecclesiastical leader, be he bishop or pastor, must be able to "summon men to faith or confirm them in a faith already living" (n. 12). Not every Christian has that kind of ability; some, indeed, seem to do the very opposite, despite their good intentions.

The bishop-pastor must be able to show the connection between "earthly goods and human institutions," on the one hand, and our quest for salvation, on the other. He must have an awareness of the meaning and implications of some of the grave questions of our day, affecting "the ownership, increase, and just distribution of material goods, peace and war, and brotherly relations among all peoples."

Many Christians are not able to make this connection and, in fact, most American Catholics, if we are to believe the 1968 Gallup poll, do not see the connection at all. The council identified this failure as "one of the more serious errors of our age" (Pastoral Constitution on the Church in the Modern World, n. 43).

The ecclesiastical leader must "present Christian doctrine in a manner corresponding to the difficulties and problems by which people are most vexatiously burdened and troubled" (n. 13). He must "strive to use the various means at hand today for making Christian doctrine known." He must see to it that adequate catechetical instruction and Christian formation are available not only to the young but "even grownups." And he must "take care that catechists be properly trained for their task."

There are, of course, many Catholics who find it very difficult, if not impossible, to adapt the Christian message to the changing circumstances of our time. Many have the attitude, in the best of faith, that what was good enough for them is certainly good enough for today. The council suggests that such Catholics, their good will notwithstanding, are not qualified for the office of bishop or pastor.

There are also many Catholics, already in the priesthood, who are not noticeably concerned about the task of adult education. Others do not exact high enough standards in the recruitment of teachers in their various educational programs. For some, two qualities are sufficient: sincerity and availability. The council indicates, however, that an ecclesiastical

178

leader must regard the task of handing on the faith, to all people at all levels, as a matter of utmost seriousness, too serious, in fact, to be left to the well-meaning but incompetent.

The bishop and pastor must be able to present the Gospel in a manner adapted to the times, showing concern for all men, believers and nonbelievers, and especially for the poor. "Bishops especially are called upon to approach men, seeking and fostering dialogue with them." These conversations are to be marked by clarity, gentleness, humility, and a "due prudence allied, however, with that trustfulness which fosters friendship" (n. 13).

Not all Catholics possess these characteristics. They cannot dialogue because they cannot listen. They are not trustful. They may be holy, sincere, kind, and willing people, but they are not qualified for positions of ecclesiastical leadership.

The Church proclaims God's Kingdom among men, not only in word, but also in sacrament. One principal way in which the Church proclaims and indeed celebrates the Kingdom's presence is through its Eucharist.

The council document states that the bishops are "the principal dispensers of the mysteries of God," that they are "the governors, promoters, and guardians of the entire liturgical life in the church committed to them. Hence, they should constantly exert themselves to have the faithful know and live the paschal mystery more deeply through the Eucharist and thus become a firmly knit body in the solidarity of Christ's love" (n. 15). Not all Catholics have sufficient liturgical sensitivity to assume such responsibility for the worship of the Church. Again, they may be holy, kind, sincere, and willing people, but they are not qualified for ecclesiastical leadership.

(B) The Church is also called upon to be a sacrament or sign of the Kingdom of God on earth. If the Church is to be a credible sign of the Kingdom, it must be a holy community, at every level of its life and existence. The bishop-pastors "should be diligent in fostering holiness among their clerics, religious, and laity, according to the special vocation of each. They should also be mindful of their obligation to give an example of holiness through charity, humility, and simplicity of life" (n. 15). On this basis, too, some people are disqualified for ecclesiastical leadership, without prejudice to the sincerity and strength of their personal faith and devotion.

(C) Finally, the Church must be an effective instrument of the Kingdom, facilitating its entrance and enabling God's presence to break into the world. The Church is a servant community, seeking how it might use its various resources for the sake of renewing society, conforming it to the will of God that there should be justice, charity, freedom, and peace. Accordingly, the bishop-pastor must "stand in the midst of his people as one who serves . . . a good shep-

180

herd who knows his sheep and whose sheep know him," a man who has the ability to "so gather and mold the whole family of his flock that everyone, conscious of his own duties, may live and work in the communion of love" (n. 16). He has the responsibility for coordinating and interconnecting all the various apostolic works, "whether catechetical, missionary, charitable, social, family, educational, or any other program serving a pastoral goal" (n. 17). It is this task of coordination which is the bishop-pastor's distinctive service of leadership.

The point of these remarks should be clear: the bishop and pastor are called to an office of community leadership; they must be judged according to that primary and central responsibility. Only those who demonstrate leadership qualities can be considered seriously for ordination or for ecclesiastical promotion after ordination.

Since the mission of the Church has been given by Christ to the whole People of God, every member of the Church must be concerned about the quality and kind of leadership he receives. However, he cannot fairly evaluate the qualifications and performance of his leaders unless there are some objective criteria. The council document provides several of these.

Indeed, "so important and weighty" is the pastoral office of bishops that the Second Vatican Council insisted that "diocesan bishops and others, regarded in law as their equals," should resign from office not only when they become *in*capable of continued service but even when they become "*less* capable of fulfilling their duties" of leadership (n. 21, italics mine).

Old age or poor health are not the only reasons for resignation. Any "serious reason" would suffice. One such reason, it seems, would be an officeholder's inability to cope psychologically, sociologically, and especially theologically with the changing conditions in both Church and world.

When the required resignation is not forthcoming, the council urges the "competent authority" to invite it, "so important and weighty" is the office of pastoral leadership in the Church.

The issue here is not petty politics or conflict of personalities. It is a matter of the effective implementation of the Church's mission. If we really believe in the importance of the Church's work, the quality of ecclesiastical leadership cannot be a subject for compromise. For too long, we have been trying to have it both ways.

And it is because we have been trying to have it both ways that a crisis is now upon the Church.

3. *The Crisis of Hope*

If the Catholic Church were ever to fall or simply wither away, I suspect that it would do so not so much for lack of faith as for lack of hope. There is a crisis of faith in the Church today, but the crisis of hope is more extensive and more deeply rooted.

Many Catholics are wondering not about what there is to believe in but about what there is to have hope in. They are not so much uneasy about the lordship of Jesus or his Real Presence in the Eucharist as they are about the viability of the Church as the herald, sign, and instrument of God's Kingdom. Why else do we hear them so often asking if it is possible to be a good Christian without belonging any longer to the Church? The question has long since lost its abstract character.

There are Catholics who have already given up on the Church because they lost hope in the possibility of its renewal. They were sure when they drifted away (few of them left with any bravado, most have gone unnoticed and unrecorded) that the Catholic Church would never ascend above its petty preoccupation with disputes about handshakes at the kiss of peace or the distribution of Communion in the hand. Some of them may have nodded knowingly, but sadly, as they read of the reports of the November, 1970, meeting of the American bishops. It has not changed, and it will not change.

On the other hand, there is no approach in a public lecture that so surely wins the sympathy and appreciation of a Catholic audience than a reaffirmation of the ideals of the Church coupled with some specific indications of signs of life and forward movement. I say this from experience: there are thousands of Catholics who want desperately to hope. They have, to paraphrase Tillich, the "will to hope."

They will listen and be reassured when told of the work of the Canon Law Society of America, for example. This organization has clearly done more for the practical reform of the Catholic Church in the United States than any other group. And yet at the November, 1970, meeting of the American Catholic bishops, some carefully constructed proposals of the Society (I have never known its proposals, at least in the past five or six years, to be other than carefully constructed) were turned aside.

These Catholic audiences will nod approvingly when informed of recent efforts, again on the part of the Canon Law Society, to widen the process by which bishops are selected. And yet they know that some of the most recent appointments, with an occasional exception, follow the usual pattern: safe men elevated by secret procedures controlled by a astonishingly small percentage of the Church's membership.

These Catholics like to hear about the trend toward the creation of diocesan and parish councils, but they eventually return home to confront the situation as it is, not as it should be.

They are genuinely pleased, I think, to hear a theologian explain and defend the specifically Catholic understanding of the Church, with its affirmation of the principle of collegiality, of papacy, and of episcopacy. But the warm moment passes and soon they are asking pointed questions, born of discouragement and disillusionment, about the pope, the bishops as a group, their own bishop, and their pastor. The theory is fine, they say, but the reality is another matter.

These Catholics will respond with interest to a critique of their own earlier and narrower views of the Church's mission, restricting it to preaching, teaching, catechesis, and worship and placing the rest—the so-called social apostolate—under the tattered umbrella of "pre-evangelization." They are delighted to be informed that the Pastoral Constitution of Vatican II referred to this breach between Christian faith and social and political responsibilities as "one of the more serious errors of our age." But then they wonder why the Church so often appears to be concerned primarily with the maintenance of its own plant (the preoccupation, however legitimate, with the salvation of the school system) and the preservation of certain of its customary life-styles and devotional habits.

To have spent time arguing about Communion in the hand is deplorable enough, these Catholics would argue, but to have voted it down, even as an option for those who prefer it, is almost beyond belief. Can a Church with that kind of leadership really be expected to unleash prophetic fire upon this earth? Can it really be expected to challenge the powers-that-be at every point, to be the spokesman of justice, the instrument of peace, the defender of freedom, the lobbyist for the poor, the bridge of reconciliation— the community of hope?

There are many Catholics who have already lost hope in the Church, and they have left. And the un-Christian cries, contorted by anger and misshapen by sickness, that follow them only confirm them in in their sad judgment that the spark of hope has indeed gone out of the Body of Christ.

There are so many other Catholics who have not lost hope, but for them the crisis of hope is real and immediate. They can be reassured a little while longer by reminders of past achievements and by our sometimes exaggerated claims of contemporary prog-ress. But in the long run only performance will give life to the rhetoric. And that is how it should be, according to the council: "By thus giving witness to the truth, we will share with others the mystery of the heavenly Father's love. As a consequence, men throughout the world will be aroused to a lively hope —the gift of the Holy Spirit—that they will finally be caught up in peace and utter happiness in that fatherland radiant with the splendor of the Lord" (Pastoral Constitution, n. 93).

The Church will be a sign of hope when it gives "witness to the truth" and it gives witness to the truth when it is fulfilling the mission given it by Christ. The function of the ordained ministry is to

186

see to it that the Church at large is faithful to its own ministry.

"Pastors also know," the Dogmatic Constitution on the Church states, "that they themselves were not meant by Christ to shoulder alone the entire saving mission of the Church toward the world. On the contrary, they understand that it is their noble duty so to shepherd the faithful. and recognize their services and charismatic gifts that all according to their proper roles may cooperate in this common undertaking with one heart. For we must all 'practice the truth in love, and so grow up in all things in him who is head, Christ. For from him the whole body . . . derives its increase to the building up of itself in love' (Eph. 4:15-16)" (n. 30).

The key problem, therefore, in this discussion as in so many others, is the question of the mission of the Church. What is the Church for? What is its task, its function, its purpose? If, indeed, the leadership responsibility of the ordained Christian means a responsibility of coordination and integration for the sake of achieving a common goal, what is that goal?

Until now, many Christians have been content to identify the mission of the Church with preaching, teaching, and worship. For Catholics, it is enough to say that the Church is the "ordinary means of salvation"; for Protestants, the Church is "the congregations of saints wherein the Gospel is rightly preached and the sacraments rightly administered."

It is little wonder that the Gallup poll in 1968 and the National Opinion Research Center survey in 1969 disclosed that most American Catholics and American Protestants oppose the involvement of their churches in matters of social and political significance. They simply cannot see the connection between Christian faith and the so-called secular sphere of life. They do not yet understand the nature and scope of the Church's task.

The Church exists not for its own sake, but for the sake of God's reign among men (=humanization, the fulfillment of all that God calls us to become). The relationship of the Church to the reign of God is the same as Christ's (see n. 5, *Lumen Gentium*):

(1) as *spokesman*   (preaching, worship, proclamation);

(2) as *embodiment*   (community of faith, hope, love); and

(3) as *facilitator*   (enabling the Kingdom to break in where there is injustice, hostility, etc.).

If that is the Church's ministry, then it is the ministry of the ordained Christian to so integrate, coordinate, and inspire that process that the Church might more effectively achieve this purpose.

Again, you can't have it both ways. You can't say, on the hand, that the Church is vital to the coming of the Kingdom of God, and then say, on the other hand, that the quality of the Church's leadership really doesn't make any difference. If the Church is simply a marching-and-chowder society, an organization which exists to cater to the religious needs of a minority of the world's population, then leadership is not crucial. So long as your principal functionnaires are kind, pleasant, uncontroversial and available, that is all that is required. On the other hand, if the Church is meant to fulfill the terms of the theological rhetoric often used to describe its life and purpose (and the Second Vatican Council used more than its share of such rhetoric), then the quality and kind of that Church's leadership is of paramount importance.

We can't have it both ways. At least not for much longer.

DISCUSSION QUESTIONS

1. In recent sociological surveys, it has been disclosed that many American priests are disenchanted with the quality of ecclesiastical leadership and are frustrated by their inability to do anything about the selection of new bishops. Do you think that leadership is the number one problem for the Church today? If so, why? If not, why not?

2. If you were writing a job description for a bishop or a pastor, what would you include in it? By

189

what standards should you evaluate the performance of a bishop or a pastor?

3. Can you think of one or two changes in the life
    and work of bishops and pastors that would im-
    prove the quality of their service in a substantial
    way?

4. Do you think that the quality of seminary train-
    ing and education is important? Do you know
    anything about it? If so, what change or changes
    would you suggest that would substantially im-
    prove the calibre of priests coming out of sem-
    inaries today?

5. Do you think that ordination should be open to
    women? If so, why? If not, why not? Do you
    think that the Church has discriminated against
    women, or at least has failed to incorporate their
    talents into the life and mission of the Church?
    If so, how do you think this has been done? If
    not, why do you think many women feel this
    way about the Church?

APPENDIX I

CONTEMPORARY QUESTIONS ABOUT
THE CATHOLIC CHURCH

Q. Our parish is considering beginning a series of discussions on the documents of Vatican II. Where do we start? Which documents should receive priority?

A. The first rule is that you should have a competent resource person. There is nothing more futile than a discussion that is little more than "shared ignorance." Besides, you would soon find that the rhetoric and terminology of the documents does not exactly titillate one's sense of literary grace. The documents tend to be formal and technical. They presuppose, to a large extent, some theological background. Therefore, someone with a theological education (not necessarily a priest however) should be either a member of the group, or "employed" by the group, on an *ad hoc* basis, as a resource in discussion. One does not simply take up the council documents and start reading, no more than one simply takes up the Bible and begins interpreting it right on the spot. Competent people have already addressed themselves to these same problems, and we cannot afford to ignore their findings and judgments.

There are several commentaries on the council documents and they vary widely in content, depth, and tone. The most scholarly commentary now available in English (and a good resource person might want to look at it) is the Herder & Herder series edited by H. Vorgrimler, *Commentary on the Documents of Vatican II*. The whole series would make a useful purchase by a parish library. Other commentaries are less ambitious, e.g., the Paulist series (Deus Books) which contain text, interpretation, and study questions. The best collection of council documents is the Abbott-Gallagher paperback edition of *The Documents of Vatican II* (America Press). This book is practically indispensable as a basic text.

191

The most important documents are these: the Dogmatic Constitution of the Church, the Pastoral Constitution on the Church in the Modern World, the Dogmatic Constitution on Divine Revelation, the Constitution on the Sacred Liturgy, and the Decree on Ecumenism.

Q.   Is it proper any longer to speak of the Roman Catholic Church as the "one, true Church of Christ?" If not, haven't we yielded to the temptation of religious indifferentism where one religion is considered to be as good as another?

A.   The expression "one, true Church of Christ" is misleading and it should be avoided. It implies that Catholics are the only real members of the Body of Christ.

The relationship between Catholics and non-Catholic Christians was a matter of some discussion in the 1940's and 1950's, particularly as the ecumenical movement among Protestants grew and as people began wondering whether or not the Catholic Church could, in good conscience, associate itself with this new quest of Christian unity. It seemed to many Catholics, including many of the Church's leaders, that participation in the ecumenical movement would imply that unity was a future goal and did not already exist in the Roman Catholic Church. Such an assumption seemed to compromise the Catholic conviction that the unity Christ desired is to be found in the Catholic Church, and that the only way to full Christian unity was through the return of all non-Catholic Christians to the Roman Catholic Church.

There was some basis for this sort of reasoning even in contemporary papal documents, such as the two encyclical letters of Pope Pius XII, *Mystici Corporis* (1943) and *Humani Generis* (1950). In the latter document the pope had written: ". . . the mystical Body of Christ and the Catholic Church in communion with Rome are one and the same thing . . ." Therefore, it was not enough that non-Catholic Christians were baptized, or reverenced the Word of God in Sacred Scripture, or celebrated some of the sacraments. They lacked one thing that was presumably absolutely essential for membership in the Body of Christ; namely, communion

192

with Rome. Thus, all non-Catholic Christians were related to the Church merely by desire *(in voto)*, which means that if they actually knew the Roman Catholic Church to be the "one, true Church of Christ," they would spontaneously join it.

On first reading the eighth article of the Second Vatican Council's Dogmatic Constitution on the Church, it seems that the council is simply reaffirming the teaching of those earlier encyclicals. The text of the constitution reads: "This (one) Church (of Christ), constituted and organized in the world as a society, *subsists in* the Catholic Church" (italics mine).

As a matter of fact, however, the phrase "subsists in" was not in the original draft of the document. Rather, it was selected as a more accurate and suitable replacement for the "is" that appeared in the first draft. The reason offered for this change was that *de facto* there do exist outside the visible boundaries of the Catholic Church genuine elements of sanctification (see, for example, the Decree of Ecumenism, n. 3). Vatican II was saying, therefore, that the means of Christian holiness are not confined to the Catholic Church, and that the Body of Christ is larger in scope and extent than the Catholic Church by itself.

One can conclude that the Body of Christ "subsists in" the Catholic Church, but one cannot say, without serious qualification, that the Body of Christ and the Catholic Church are simply "one and the same thing." Other Christians, who do not belong to the Catholic Church, share in the life of Christ's Body, even though the degree of such participation may differ from one Christian community to another, or from individual to individual.

One final comment: it is also wrong to speak of Catholics and non-Catholic Christians as if they belong to different "religions." There are different denominations and different traditions, but all Christians profess and practice the same religion. The same reasoning would apply to the custom of referring to non-Catholic Christians as holding to a different "faith." Thus, a Protestant who becomes a Catholic is described sometimes as one who "accepts the faith." This is not only demeaning to the non-Catholic Christian community in question, but it is also theologically inaccurate. There is only one Lord, one faith, and one baptism (Ephesians 4:5-6). If a person accepts Jesus of Nazareth as the Lord, he is a Christian and he shares the same basic faith as a Catholic who makes the same profession about Jesus.

Therefore, when one moves from one community to another within the Body of Christ, he does not embrace a different faith (unless, in his previous situation, he did not accept the Lordship of Jesus and now he does). By the same token, were a Catholic to shift his own place within the Body of Christ (without renouncing faith in the Lord, and faith in his presence in the Christian community and in its sacraments), one cannot responsibly speak of that Catholic as one who has "lost the faith." I am not urging the latter course, nor making light of its consequences or implications. But we should be aware that not all of our "common-sense theology" is always accurate. Sometimes it is wrong, and Christian respect for persons is often lost in the process.

Q. *Is there any definition of the Church that all Christians, or at least all Catholics, agree upon?*

A. The Church has been defined in various ways: as the Body of Christ, the People of God, the new Israel, the community of the elect, the sacrament of Christ, the congregation of saints wherein the Gospel is rightly preached and the sacraments rightly celebrated, and so forth. Although the Second Vatican Council speaks constantly of the Church, nowhere does it offer a single, hard-and-fast definition which must be accepted by all Catholics without modification.

This does not mean, however, that we are at a complete loss. There are, in fact, certain elements for a definition that most Christians should be able to agree upon. These elements are drawn from various sources: principally from the Bible, doctrine, and theology.

The Church is the community of those who are called to acknowledge the Lordship of Jesus, who ratify that faith sacramentally, and who commit themselves thereby to membership and mission for the sake of the Kingdom of God in history.

The Church is, first of all, a community. It is people. It is not, in the first instance, an organization, or a means of salvation. It is not the hierarchy or the clergy. The Church is a community. (Note, for example, that the chapter on the People of God in the Dogmatic Constitution on the Church comes before, not after, the chapter on the hierarchy. This particular arrangement, however, was not achieved without a serious struggle at the council).

But the Church is not simply a community. It is not just people. It is a special kind of community. It is a particular group of people who differ from other people in one important respect: Christians are those who affirm that the meaning and hope of human existence and of history itself reside in Jesus of Nazareth, whom God has raised up for our salvation.

This, and this alone, is what makes Christians different from the rest of mankind. Not that Christians are holier than other people. Not that Christians believe in God and give him due worship. Not that Christians believe in the brotherhood of man. Not that Christians believe in social justice and in the service of mankind. For these are things that Christians have in common with other religious and even nonreligious people.

What distinguishes the Christian from the non-Christian, and the Church from the rest of mankind, is the conviction and the faith that Jesus of Nazareth is the Lord, that he, and he alone, is the pattern and ground of all life. That what we call good and human, we call good and human because it participates in the reality of him. And what we call evil and inhuman, we call evil and inhuman because it recedes from, or rejects, the reality embodied in Jesus of Nazareth.

195

But the Church not only affirms the Lordship of Jesus, it actively and joyfully celebrates it. The Church is not just a group of people sharing a common view of history, arising more or less from a common view of Jesus of Nazareth. Christian faith is not, in other words, simply a philosophy of life. It is rather a way of life that one embraces precisely insofar as he enters the company of Jesus's disciples. Faith is offered through community, and it is embraced and lived in community. One responds to preaching (Romans 10:14-17), repents of his sins, and is baptized (Acts 2:38). From that time on, he devotes himself "to the apostles' teaching and fellowship, to the breaking of the bread and the prayers" (Acts 2:42).

But the Church is not only a community which acknowledges and sacramentally celebrates the Lordship of Jesus. It seeks also to realize his Lordship throughout the whole world, to bring the reign of God to all men and to all human institutions, in order that there might be justice and peace, charity and righteousness. Whatever definition of the Church we may finally agree upon, it must incorporate in some way the principle that the Church is a servant community, following in the footsteps of its founder, the Suffering Servant of God (see Mark 10:45, and the Pastoral Constitution on the Church in the Modern World, n. 3). The Church exists as herald, sign, and instrument of God's Kingdom on earth. The Church, indeed, has no meaning apart from its relationship to the Kingdom of God.

Q. You wouldn't be satisfied, then, with definitions which identified the Church with the human community at large? Couldn't one say that the Church is wherever the Spirit happens to be, wherever the struggle against dehumanization is taking place, wherever people are becoming friends?

A. No. These definitions tend to equate the Church with the Kingdom of God. It is to be hoped, of course, that the Church and the Kingdom of God overlap. We have a right to expect, that is, a fuller flowering of the Gospel among those people who presume to preach it and to celebrate it publicly. The Church should be recognized as the initial budding forth of the Kingdom on earth (see the Dogmatic Constitution on the Church, n. 5). But the Church and the Kingdom are not one and the same reality. Where you have the Church, you don't necessarily have the Kingdom; and where you have the Kingdom, you don't necessarily have the Church either.

Q. Does the Second Vatican Council endorse the so-called "new morality"?

A. If by the "new morality" one means an emphasis on personal responsibility rather than the mere observance of laws, then the council did endorse the "new morality:"

"In fidelity to conscience, Christians are joined with the rest of men in the search for truth, and for the genuine solution to the numerous problems which arise in the life of individuals and from social relationships . . . . Only in freedom can man direct himself toward goodness" (Pastoral Constitution on the Church in the Modern World, n. 16-17).

If by the "new morality" one means a recognition that love of God and love of neighbor are radically inseparable (i.e., that one takes his stand for or against God on the basis of his stand for or against his fellow man, whether it be his wife or husband, his child or parent, his relative or friend, his acquaintance or co-worker, or whether it be someone he has never met but who, as a fellow human being in need, has a real moral claim upon him), then the council did endorse it:

"Love for God and neighbor is the first and greatest commandment. Sacred Scripture, however, teaches us that the love of God cannot be separated from love of neighbor: 'If there is any other commandment, it is summed up in this saying, Thou shalt love thy neighbor as thyself . . . Love therefore is the fulfillment of the Law (Rom 13:9-10; cf. 1 Jn 4:20). To men growing daily more dependent on one another, and to a world becoming more unified every day, this truth proves to be of paramount importance" (Pastoral Constitution, n. 24).

If by the "new morality" one means leaving behind a narrowly individualistic view of Christianity and adopting instead a more social, community-minded view, then the council did endorse it:

"Man's social nature makes it evident that the progress of the human person and the advance of society itself hinge on each other . . . . Every day human interdependence grows more tightly drawn and spreads by degrees over the whole world . . . . God did not create man for life in isolation, but for the formation of social unity . . . . So from the beginning of salvation history He has chosen men not just as individuals but as members of a certain community . . . . This solidarity must be constantly increased until that day on which it will be brought to perfection" (n. 25, 26, and 32).

If by the "new morality" one means a greater sensitivity to social and political issues, toward the responsibility of every human being and especially of every Christian to work for the reform of the social order and not only for the salvation of one's own soul, then the council did endorse it:

"This social order requires constant improvement. It must be founded on truth, built on justice, and animated by love; in freedom it should grow every day toward a more humane balance . . . . Profound and rapid changes make it particularly urgent that no one, ignoring the trend of events or drugged by laziness, content himself with a merely individualistic morality. It grows increasingly true that the obligations of justice and love are fulfilled only if each person, contributing to the common good, according to his own abilities and the needs of others, also promotes and assists the public and private institutions dedicated to bettering the conditions of human life" (n. 26 and 30).

If, however, one means by the "new morality" a state of mind that rejects the reality of sin, ignores the dignity of the human person and of human life, makes light of the need for contrition and penance, or tends to identify the Kingdom of God with the handiwork of man alone, then one will look in vain throughtout the council documents for any such endorsement.

The council supports freedom of conscience, but it is not indifferent to the manner in which one forms his conscience. It does not deny those abiding values by which man determines how he must act and why (see n. 16-17).

The council insists that love of God and love of neighbor are inseparable, but it does not suggest that "God" *is* our neighbor (see n. 19-21, on atheism).

The council urges us to see our social and communitarian responsibilities and not to look upon the Christian life as a matter of individual concern alone, but it does not thereby disregard the reverence due each human person and each human life (e.g., n. 27).

The council indicates that there is a close connection between the coming of the Kingdom of God and our work here and now in the political order, but it does not teach that the Kingdom of God will be the handiwork of man, created by men, for men (see n. 39).

Whether we call it the "new morality" or not, the substance of the council's teachings on the Christian life is a matter of major importance. Catholics, and particularly those with pastoral responsibility, cannot afford to ignore it.

Q. *We were always taught that the religious life is superior to the married state. Marriage was never downgraded, of course. Christ, after all, made it a sacrament. But those who aspired to the priesthood or to membership in a religious community were regarded as seeking the highest Christian vocation. Is this still the thinking of the Church? Certainly the younger generation doesn't accept this line of thought.*

A. Even though the Council of Trent emphasized the sacramental dignity of marriage, it also condemned those who maintained that "the married state is preferable to that of virginity or celibacy and that it is not better and more blessed to continue in the state of virginity or celibacy than to enter on the state of matrimony."

199

Trent offered several New Testament texts as supporting evidence: Mt. 19:11 f., 1 Cor. 7:25 f., 38, and 40. The view was reaffirmed by Pope Pius XII in his encyclical letter, *Sacra Virginitas,* in 1954. It is probably fair to say that most Catholics, and certainly those in the over-30 generation, would regard this as common and indisputable Catholic teaching.

The Second Vatican Council does not explicitly repudiate those earlier papal and conciliar statements and it comes closest to reaffirming them in its Decree on Priestly Formation (n. 10).

However, there is also some indication, specifically in the Dogmatic Constitution on the Church, that the council wished to move away from the idea that only those Christians who live a celibate life can really serve God with an undivided heart: "All of Christ's followers, therefore, are invited and bound to pursue holiness and the perfect fulfillment of their proper state" (n. 42). Indeed, the chapter from which this line is taken is entitled "The Call of the Whole Church to Holiness." The theme is developed most fully in article 40.

Why is it that so many lay people today resist any reinterpretation or modification of the earlier view that the religious state is preferable to their own? Is it because they do not like to see the magisterium of the Church change its mind on various key issues and thereby increase the sense of uncertainty and confusion among the faithful? Or is their own experience of marriage so unsatisfactory that they assume the unmarried state to be superior, almost by a process of elimination?

Perhaps this is true in some cases. But it seems that many of the Catholic laity are still happy with the traditional view (namely, that the religious life is objectively superior to the married state) because they understand it to mean that only the religious and the priests are really bound to live the Christian life to its fullest. Only priests, monks, brothers, and nuns are seriously expected to be people of prayer, reflection, sacrifice, and penance. It is almost as if the laity share vicariously in the benefits which accrue from the spiritual activities and practices of the religious.

The Second Vatican Council, without resolving the issue of the relative merits of celibacy and marriage, places the burden of perfect holiness where it belongs: on the whole Church. No one is exempt. If some Christians can more readily and effectively proclaim, signify, and facilitate God's Kingdom by a life of celibacy, then so be it. Most Christians will find, however, that their quest of God's Kingdom among men will be supported and realized from within the married state.

There are no "super-Christians." There are no people whose special job is to keep God happy, to hold back the arm of vengeance, while the rest go about their own business. All men are equal in God's sight, and all men will be judged by the very same criteria: "You, therefore, must be perfect, as your heavenly Father is perfect" (Mt. 5:48).

Q. Does this mean that celibacy is not an essential requirement for the priesthood or the religious life?

A. Celibacy is, at present, an essential *legal* requirement for the priesthood and religious life. And there are excellent reasons— in the New Testament, the Fathers of the Church, the earlier councils, and in theology—for a celibate priesthood, freely chosen. But there is no theological, doctrinal or biblical argument for *obligatory* celibacy.

Celibacy was not always a requirement for ordination in the Catholic Church. Indeed, there are segments of the Catholic Church which have a married clergy. If the law is changed, it will not involve a change of doctrine or a change of theology. It will be a change of legal discipline only.

Q. In the early days of the World Council of Churches, Catholic participation was practically nonexistent. If I recall correctly, such participation was rejected both by the conservative wing of the World Council and by the Vatican itself. Recent meetings of the WCC have been attended by official Catholic observers. Is there any theological reason why the Catholic Church cannot be a full member of the World Council?

A. In my judgment, no. The earlier opposition to Catholic participation in the WCC was based on the premise that the Catholic Church is the "one, true Church of Christ" and that the only path to Christian unity is one of *return* to the Catholic Church. For the Catholic Church to enter a world organization dedicated to *seeking* Christian unity would have been a denial of her belief that such unity already existed within her own bosom and that Protestants and others must eventually become Catholics. (Others opposed Catholic membership on the mistaken notion that the WCC was itself a kind of super-church, rather than a forum of ecumenical dialogue and collaboration.)

It seems to me, however, that the expression "one, true Church of Christ," with all that it has traditionally implied, is misleading, and it tends to slur the Christian integrity of non-Catholic Christians. The Body of Christ is larger than the Roman Catholic Church (see the Dogmatic Constitution on the Church, n. 8). Catholics are not the only real Christians (see n. 15). To the degree that non-Catholic Christians are affiliated with the Body of Christ, to that same degree are they already sharers in whatever unity has been given by the Holy Spirit.

The concern of the Second Vatican Council and the World Council of Churches is basically the same: that all Christians might be brought together in fuller unity in order that the entire Body of Christ might be a credible spokesman, sign, and instrument of God's Kingdom on earth. If Catholic participation in the WCC would advance the cause of Christian unity and mission, then such participation should be encouraged. Ecumenists today seem to think that this is, indeed, the case.

Q. *It has been suggested by some theologians, canon lawyers, and others, that the present practice for the selection of bishops should be set aside in favor of a system which allows for broader participation by clergy and laity alike. This may make some sense to those of us who live in a democratic society, but can we really change the present system of episco-*

pal appointment without violating the essential nature of the Church as a monarchical institution?

A. Your fundamental assumption is wrong. The Church is a collegial, not a monarchical, institution. Furthermore, the whole Church—clergy, religious, and laity alike—has received the mission to proclaim, signify, and bring about the Kingdom of God among men (see especially chapters II and IV, the Dogmatic Constitution on the Church). Because all baptized Christians are incorporated into the People of God, each has some basic responsibility for the kind and quality of the Church's leadership. There is, in fact, an ancient canonical principle: "He who governs all should be elected by all."

A recent Canon Law Society of America symposium made such a recommendation: "The principle of coresponsibility, the dignity and freedom of persons, the rights of Christians, and the longstanding tradition of Church order all demand the meaningful participation of the whole community in the selection of its leaders and the formulation of laws affecting its life."

In some dioceses the clergy has already been asked to express its preference regarding future episcopal appointments, but such instances are on an *ad hoc* basis and have no clearly defined canonical force. What seems clear enough in principle, therefore, remains as yet unsettled in practice. The matter of wider practical implementation, however, is now under study.

See *The Choosing of Bishops,* edited by W. Bassett, Hartford: The Canon Law Society of America, 1971.

Q. I know of some Catholics who encourage their Protestant friends to receive Holy Communion from time to time. I have heard about so-called ecumenical eucharists celebrated in homes. I must admit that this is rather disturbing to me and some of my friends. How can a Protestant receive Communion at a Catholic Mass?

A. According to present Church law, he may not. Will there ever come a time when intercommunion will be approved by the Catholic Church, at least on special occasions? I think so. Several theological committees have been discussing this question in the past three or four years (e.g., Catholic-Lutheran, Catholic-Episcopalian, Catholic-Presbyterian, Catholic-Disciples of Christ, and Catholic-Eastern Orthodox). Of these groups, only the Catholic-Orthodox committee has issued a discouraging report on the immediate possibilities of intercommunion involving their respective churches.

This is a controversial matter, I know. It is easily open to misinterpretation. But Catholics should not be led to believe that intercommunion is an absolute impossibility, something which can never be justified and, therefore, never will happen. If this impression is allowed to stand, and if at some future time the Catholic Church does accept intercommunion on a limited basis, we'll have the same kind of "weeping and gnashing of teeth" among sincere, traditional Catholics that we have already experienced on other important issues.

Article 8 of the Decree on Ecumenism puts the issue succinctly: "As for common worship, however, it may not be regarded as a means to be used indiscriminately for the restoration of unity among Christians. Such worship depends chiefly on two principles: it should signify the unity of the Church; it should provide a sharing in the means of grace. The fact that it should signify unity generally rules out common worship. Yet the gaining of a needed grace sometimes commends it."

Q. *At the last meeting of our Parish Council, just before the summer recess, our pastor asked us if we should continue as a group or if we should disband. Some of us were very disturbed by this question because it confirmed our suspicions about his attitude toward the council. He regards it as a kind of luxury the parish can do without; at best, a parish discussion club over which he deigns to preside. And yet we're probably better off than many of our neighbors. Three of the surrounding parishes have no Parish Councils at all. Is it any surprise that many of the laity are discouraged and really wonder about the possibility of reform so long as these attitudes continue to prevail among so many of the clergy?*

A. The existence of parish councils is not a matter of ecclesiastical politics alone. There are theological issues and principles at stake here. The Church is not, in the first instance, a mechanism of salvation presided over by certain men who hold the key to the means of salvation. The Church is people. The Second Vatican Council calls it the very "People of God."

Although the Christian community has structure (see, for example, chapter III of the Dogmatic Constitution on the Church), there are no elites, on the one hand, or second class-citizens, on the other. Everything which the council said about the People of God in chapter II of the Dogmatic Constitution on the Church it meant to apply equally to clergy, religious, and laity alike (see n. 30).

Furthermore, all members of the Church share the mission which Christ gave to the whole Church. The laity do not simply assist the hierarchy or the clergy in the fulfillment of the multiple tasks of the Church. The laity participates in the very saving mission of Christ himself, and this has been communicated to the laity in the sacraments, especially in Baptism and Confirmation (n. 33).

The apostolate of the Church belongs to absolutely every Christian. "Upon all the laity, therefore, rests the noble duty of working to extend the divine plan of salvation ever increasingly to all men of each epoch and in every land. Consequently, let every opportunity be given them so that, according to their abilities and the needs of the times, they may zealously participate in the saving work of the Church" (n. 33).

Those who oppose the establishment of parish councils (or of diocesan and national pastoral councils) betray a certain notion of the Church which cannot be supported by contemporary theology or by the documents of the Second Vatican Council. And this would have to apply as well to those who have allowed only "rubber-stamp" councils to form. If all the people in a given eucharistic community are not allowed to participate meaningfully in the life and work of the Church, then something essential is lacking to that particular community. Principally, it is a sense of what the Church is, and what it's for.

Q. *My parish has experienced a rather upsetting change of priests. We had previously been a progressive parish, and our pastor and assistant pastor were both ardent proponents of Vatican II and its entire view of Christianity. Their replacements are both conservative and vocally opposed to almost all change. Our CCD teachers face the worst difficulty in this change of leadership. After much effort and patience in explaining such changes as the delay of First Confession until three years after First Communion, the elimination of the altar rail, the introduction of a Folk Mass, and so forth, our teachers are now faced with the unhappy task of explaining why all of these changes have now been cancelled and whey we've had to return to the old way in every instance. How do we progress so far in the understanding of the externals of our religion and then be expected to retrace all of our steps? What is the catechist supposed to do? Before you misunderstand the situation, you should know that the pastor has no communication with the people. He refuses to discuss anything with anyone who seems the least bit progressive, and the CCD is considered a contaminating influence in the parish. Some have "solved" the problem by going to other parishes. If there is a way to fight for these changes and stay within the parish community, this would be preferred. What can you suggest?*

A. The situation is not uncommon today. Indeed, it frequently happens in reverse, when an insensitive progressive team replaces a long-established conservative administration. Undoubtedly, many readers have experienced both kinds of situations. Neither of them is very pleasant, and they are almost never pastorally productive.

A bishop (or personnel board) really ought to foresee situations like this one. If the bishop (or personnel board) still wants to make this change, he must be satisfied that the new leadership is compassionate, patient, and tolerant. The new pastor will have to be prepared to consult with his parish community before making changes which might seriously upset a significant portion of the people. As the Second Vatican Council reminded us, pastors "were not meant by Christ to shoulder alone the entire saving mission of the Church toward the world. On the contrary, they (must) understand that it is their noble duty so to shepherd the faithful and recognize their services and charismatic gifts in this common undertaking with one heart" (Dogmatic Constitution on the Church, n. 30).

If, as you say, the pastor simply refuses to enter into dialogue about his apparent rollback policy, you still have several remaining options: (1) Bring the whole matter before the Parish Council. (2) Seek advice and direction from the diocesan director of the Confraternity of Christian Doctrine. (3) Call the matter to the attention of the Priests' Senate, in order to keep this group closely informed of various problems within the diocese. (4) Register a formal complaint with the bishop and/or personnel board of the diocese.

The situation is indeed bleak in your diocese if you receive neither assistance nor encouragement from any one of these sources. Should this be the case, you are left with your final option as a practicing Catholic: (a) stay in the parish with the resolve to do whatever you can to implement the teachings and spirit of Vatican II, hoping all the while for yet another change in leadership; or (b) seek out some other eucharistic community where you can worship God and function as a Christian without pastoral obstruction. Since there is nothing intrinsically sacred about the residential parish (i.e., a eucharistic community formed according to neighborhood lines rather than common-interest lines, such as a collegiate or professional group), the second of the two options should not be discounted summarily as a form of surrender or escape.

Q. Whenever I've discussed the Pentecostal movement with Catholic theologians, they seem little interested in it. Some dismiss it entirely. Isn't the Church ignoring a great work of the Holy Spirit? Shouldn't we be encouraging people to affiliate with this movement?

A.   Catholic Pentecostalism is a relatively new phenomenon in the Catholic Church. It became a unified movement in February, 1967, at Duquesne University in Pittsburgh. From there it spread to the University of Notre Dame, the Newman Center at the University of Michigan, and then to several other places throughout the country. However, its main concentration has been in the Midwest.

The apparent lack of interest on the part of Catholic theologians might be attributed to the novelty of the movement and to the scarcity of research data. The most serious study of Catholic Pentecostalism (also referred to as "charismatic renewal") has been done by Father Kilian McDonnell, O.S.B., of the Institute for Ecumenical and Cultural Research at Collegeville, Minnesota. A summary of his findings are available in the winter, 1970, issue of *Dialog* magazine (pp. 55-54) and are reprinted in pamphlet form *(Catholic Pentecostalisms Problems in Evaluation)* by Dove Publications, Pecos, New Mexico, 87552.

A committee of the Catholic bishops of the United States recently made a special study of the movement, issuing a brief report at the Washington meeting of the American bishops in November, 1969. The tone of the report was cautiously positive: "It seems to be too soon to draw definitive conclusions regarding the phenomenon and more scholarly research is needed . . . . It must be admitted that theologically the movement has legitimate reasons for existence . . . . Perhaps our most prudent way to judge the validity of the claims of the Pentecostal Movement is to observe the effects on those who participate in the prayer meetings . . . . It is the conclusion of the Committee on Doctrine that the movement should at this point not be inhibited but allowed to develop . . . . We must be on guard that they avoid the mistakes of classic Pentecostalism. It must be recognized that in our culture there is a tendency to substitute religious experience for religious doctrine."

Among the "mistakes of classic Pentecostalism" are: anti-intellectualism, a fundamentalist interpretation of Sacred Scripture, a tendency toward emotionalism, and an indifference to the social and political dimensions of Christian responsibility. Defenders of Catholic Pentecostalism, such as Father Edward D. O'Connor, C.S.C., of the University of Notre Dame, insist that such defects do not characterize the contemporary "charismatic renewal" within the Catholic Church, although he would admit that each of these defects can be found here and there throughout the movement.

For recent literature on the subject see Father O'Connor's *The Pentecostal Movement in the Catholic Church*, Notre Dame: Ave Maria Press, 1971, and the spring, 1971, issue of *Theology Digest*, pp. 46-57.

Q. The recent capture of Father Daniel Berrigan after many weeks as a fugitive from justice raises a question in my mind: Has there been a change in Catholic moral theology to the effect that civil disobedience has become acceptable Christian behavior? Are his actions heroic or scandalous?

A. In its Decree on the Bishops' Pastoral Office in the Church, the Second Vatican Council argued that bishops have a responsibility to "advocate obedience to just laws and reverence for legitimately constituted authority" (n. 19). It is precisely the justice and legitimacy of the American political system which Father Berrigan and others have called into question, because of this country's extended involvement in military operations in Vietnam. If he is right in his assessment of these political realities, his actions—by hindsight at least—will appear to have been prophetic in the classical sense. If he is wrong, then he is open to the charge (which some have already made) of arrogance and self-righteous moralism. I happen to support the prophetic thesis. Others may legitimately disagree. I don't think the council or contemporary moral theology offer any clear-cut guidance on this issue. It is a matter of a prudential judgment fashioned, presumably, out of the context of the Gospel of Jesus Christ.

Q. *I've heard it said that reunion will come more quickly with the Protestants than with the Orthodox. This seems highly unlikely because the Orthodox believe almost as much as we Catholics. The only doctrine of faith they don't accept is the supremacy and infallibility of the pope. Does this make any sense?*

A. Given the traditional framework of thought adopted for so long by so many Catholics, your attitude makes eminently good sense. The Orthodox churches are "closer" to the Catholic Church because they believe in more "Catholic truths" than any of the other Christian communities, including the Anglicans.

As a matter of fact, however, the greatest resistance to intercommunion is is coming not from Catholic-Lutheran, or Catholic-Episcopalian, or Catholic-Presbyterian, or Catholic-Disciples of Christ dialogues, but rather from the Catholic-Orthodox dialogue on the Eucharist. One should be very careful about general, sweeping statements, of course. However, there *are* Catholic theologians who are closer to traditional Protestant theologians on the question of the nature and mission of the Church, for example, than they are to various Orthodox theologians. Christian truth is neither numerical nor quantitative. It is entirely possible that the judgment you cite is correct; namely, that reunion between Catholics and (some) Protestants will come before a Catholic-Orthodox reunion.

Q. *The National Black Sisters' Conference held its third annual conference recently at the University of Notre Dame. I was disturbed to hear these good sisters making very serious charges against their own Church. Isn't something wrong when a Catholic nun can say that Our Holy Mother, the Church, is "a racist institution?"*

A. Undoubtedly, there *is* something wrong, but we can't automatically assume that it's the sister and not the Church that's at fault.

210

Of course, no Catholic likes to hear his Church attacked as a racist, and least of all a white Catholic. But whether we accept this blanket condemnation or not, it is difficult to avoid the truth that the Catholic Church in the United States has failed to elicit the trust and support of the overwhelming majority of black citizens in this nation.

These black sisters, and other black Catholics as well, have something to say to the rest of the American Catholic community: that the Catholic parochial school system has often, unintentionally or not, served as a refuge for white Catholics from integrated situations; that white American Catholics did not become seriously interested in the problem of drug addiction until it began afflicting their own sons and daughters; that white American Catholics are usually no different from any other white Americans in their response to the desire of blacks to purchase homes in white neighborhoods; that white American Catholics harbor the same prejudices and resentments against blacks (e.g., that all blacks are poor because they are lazy) that other white Americans have; and that Catholic religious communities have failed to provide an atmosphere conducive to the preservation of black values and black culture and, therefore, have prevented many black sisters and priests from rising to positions of leadership in the Church.

The truth of the last charge is particularly sharp. Oftentimes, when black men and women entered Catholic religious communities, the ideals of religious life with which they were presented contradicted some of the highest values of black culture. Thus, the young postulant or seminarian was enjoined to control his emotions, to adhere to rigid schedules, and to downgrade the physical side of life. "Entering an order," one of the conference delegates said, "meant ceasing to be black and looking on what you grew up with as uncouth."

The Second Vatican Council has challenged the assumption that Church unity comes only through complete uniformity. Legitimate differences (i.e., differences which do not go to the heart of the Christian faith) "do not hinder unity but rather contribute toward it" (Dogmatic Constitution on the Church, n. 13). Whatever is good in the cultures of diverse peoples must be preserved (n. 17). Indeed, we must always foster within the Church "mutual esteem, reverence, and harmony, through the full recognition of lawful diversity" (Pastoral Constitution on the Church in the Modern World, n. 92).

Q. How authoritative are the documents of the Second Vatican Council? I understand that they are not intended to be infallible. Does this mean that the average Catholic can take them or leave them, depending upon his personal whims?

A. It is true that the Second Vatican Council never invoked the gift of infallibility in promulgating its various constitutions, decrees, and declarations. It is not true, however, that the documents lack all ecclesiastical authority thereby.

If this were the case, Catholics would only have to take seriously infallible statements of the Church. And such statements are decidedly few in number. Indeed, since the proclamation of the dogma of papal infallibility at the First Vatican Council a hundred years ago, there has been only one exercise of this prerogative; namely, in the definition of the Blessed Mother's Assumption.

At their most authoritative level, the documents of Vatican II are in the category of "Catholic doctrine." They represent the teaching of the Church's magisterium in such wise that a Catholic must have good and solid reasons for disagreeing with such teachings. Much of the material in the documents of various ecumenical councils, as well as some material contained in papal encyclicals, falls into this category.

We should remember, however, that the attribution of the term "Catholic doctrine" to a particular teaching is itself a theological judgment, and, as such, the judgment is subject to later revision.

Q. As a Catholic laywoman, I was encouraged and im·pressed by the recent actions of the pope in naming both St. Theresa of Avila and St. Catherine of Siena Doctors of the Church. According to the various news reports, these are the first women in the history of the Church to be so honored. One item, however, distressed me very much. Vatican Radio, in commenting on the delay in conferring this title of Doctor upon these two saints, said that the authorities of the Church had to proceed very cautiously because it was "necessary to solve the question of whether the charisms of the word, of knowledge and of wisdom were or were not granted to women." Vatican Radio cited the generally unfavorable attitude of St. Paul and St. Thomas Aquinas toward women. I should have assumed that such attitudes have long since been dismissed as culturally-conditioned. Do you really think that perhaps the Holy Spirit speaks more frequently to men than to women?

A. No. However, it will probably take a long time before this anti-feminist bias is thoroughly uprooted from the consciousness of the Catholic Church. There is too much evidence for it in too many areas of Church history, beginning even with the New Testament itself.

Your suggestion that such a bias is more cultural than theological is correct. Indeed, there is no possible theological justification for the belief that the revelation of God or the charisms of his Spirit are directed primarily toward men and only rarely toward women.

The fact that men have politically dominated the Church during most of its lifetime is no theological argument on behalf of their religious superiority. Rather it is testimony to the stronger pull of cultural over against theological forces in shaping the mentality and policies of ecclesiastical life.

Fortunately, the tide has begun to turn, anticipated in part by the late Pope John XXIII's encyclical letter, *Peace on Earth* (1963), wherein he referred to the emerging influence of women as one of the major, positive trends of our age (para. 41).

WHO IS A CATHOLIC?

When the Second Vatican Council spoke on the question of women in society and in the Church, the council consistently argued on behalf of equality of rights for women and of a wider participation by women in the various fields of the Church's apostolate (see, for example, the Decree on the Apostolate of the Laity, n. 9, and the Pastoral Constitution on the Church in the Modern World, n. 9, 29, and 60).

It should be pointed out, however, that the council itself established a less than enviable performance record. Over the entire four years of the council's life (1962-5), there were never more than twelve laywomen and ten religious women involved in the proceedings, in the role of auditors (auditrices).

Q. *Ever since the close of the Second Vatican Council in 1965, many dioceses throughout the country have established senates of priests to assist the bishop in caring for the Catholic people committed to him. More recently there has been some movement in the direction of establishing parish, diocesan, and even national councils, involving laity as well as clergy anr religious. This all sounds very fine in theory, but in practice can't the pastor or bishop do exactly as he pleases? What real authority can such councils ever hope to achieve?*

A. There is no overriding theological reason why such councils could not enjoy full deliberative authority, in union with the pastor or bishop. The mission of the Church is the responsibility of the whole People of God (see the Dogmatic Constitution on the Church, n. 30). If all are responsible for the work of the Church, then all—at least in principle—must share in the formulation of policies and laws which are designed to realize and to fulfill that work.

The laity and so-called "lower clergy" do not participate only in the mission of the hierarchy but rather "in the saving mission of the Church itself. Through their baptism and confirmation, all are commissioned to that apostolate by the Lord Himself" (n. 33).

Why is it, then, that senates of priests and parish or diocesan councils are always regarded as having only consultative, not deliberative, power? Why are most, if not all, of them established as purely advisory groups, without prejudice to the final authority of the pastor or bishop?

The reason is that law usually reflects the theology upon which it is based. When the Code of Canon Law was produced more than fifty years ago, it was generally assumed that the Church is an absolute monarchy, with the pope at the top of the pyramid. The legal structure of the Code embodies that basic assumption. For all practical purposes, a bishop enjoys the same kind of monarchial authority in his own diocese and a pastor, on a much lesser scale, in his own parish.

Under the multiple impact of the ecumenical, biblical, and liturgical movements, Catholic theology began to modify its understanding of the nature and mission of the Church. The documents of the Second Vatican Council reveal some of the principal achievements of post-World War II Catholic thought: The Church is the People of God. All are responsible for the mission of the Church. The Church is a collegial, not monarchical, reality. And so forth.

As the theology of Vatican II seeps into the consciousness of Catholic people in general and Catholic lawmakers in particular, we shall all experience a basic structural change in the life and work of the Catholic Church. If we are to judge by the extraordinarily perceptive and productive efforts of the Canon Law Society of America over the last several years, we can safely predict that these constructive reforms are not beyond the realm of possibility.

Q. Is it possible for someone to be in the Kingdom of God without being in the Church? Suppose a Catholic decided that he could work more effectively for the cause of God's Kingdom outside the Church than inside the Church. Would he be justified in leaving the Church?

A. If the Church and the Kingdom of God were one and the same reality, it would be impossible for one to be in the

215

Kingdom without being in the Church. However, the Kingdom and the Church are not exactly coextensive. They may indeed overlap, but they are not one and the same thing. There is no biblical support for the earlier assumption that the Church and the Kingdom are identical (see, for example, Father Rudolf Schnackenburg's *God's Rule and Kingdom*, Nelson, 1963, pp. 233-4).

It is possible, therefore, for one to be within the Kingdom of God without, at the same time, being an explicit member of the Church. It is also possible for a person to be in the Church without, at the same time, being within the Kingdom.

The relationship of Church and Kingdom has been captured in a short formula by St. Augustine: "Many whom God has the Church does not have, and many whom the Church has God does not have" (cited by Karl Rahner, S.J., in *Christian Commitment*, Sheed & Ward, 1963, p. 35). That is, many who are in the Kingdom are not in the Church, and many who are in the Church are not in the Kingdom.

According to responsible commentators (I have in mind especially Canon Charles Moeller, an official of the Congregation for the Doctrine of the Faith), article 5 of the Dogmatic Constitution on the Church was added to the document almost at the last minute, before final approval, in order to counteract a residual spirit of triumphalism. (Theologically, "triumphalism" refers to the tendency to equate the Church with the Kingdom of God and then to draw various pastoral conclusions therefrom.)

Article 5 speaks of the Church as the "initial budding forth of that Kingdom" but it refuses to identify the two realities. On the contrary, the constitution states that the Church is straining now "toward the consummation of the Kingdom" at the end of history.

Finally, one might point to the parable of the sheep and the goats in the twenty-fifth chapter of St. Matthew's Gospel where we are told that it is possible for someone to accept or to reject Christ without being explicitly aware of him ("When did I see thee hungry . . . ?") To be *explicitly* aware of Christ is to be in the Church.

Would a Catholic be justified in leaving the Church if he decided that he could work more effectively for the Kingdom outside than inside? This question recurs frequently today. Perhaps the American Catholic community is still feeling the shock waves of the dramatic departure of Charles Davis in December, 1966. Unfortunately, many pose this question without a clear enough understanding of the nature and mission of the Church.

A Christian is different from a non-Christian because the Christian affirms something about Jesus of Nazareth which the non-Christian does not affirm; namely, that Jesus of Nazareth is the Lord, that he is "the key, the focal point, and the goal of all human history" (Pastoral Constitution on the Church in the Modern World, n. 10).

Therefore, the Church is that portion of mankind which is called to acknowledge the Lordship of Jesus and to fulfill the mission which Jesus himself came to realize: the proclamation, signification, and facilitation of God's Kingdom among men. The Church, like Jesus, exists to announce the coming of the Kingdom, to be a sign of its presence in history, and to usher in the Kingdom through its various good works (see again the fifth article of the Dogmatic Constitution on the Church).

If a Catholic, or any Christian for that matter, still believes in the Lordship of Jesus and in the mission of the community which confesses his name, then he is not free to work apart from the Church for the sake of the Kingdom. To believe in the Lordship of Jesus is to be implicated already in the community which keeps his memory alive.

When people raise this question of leaving the Church in order to do God's work more effectively, they are usually thinking of certain canonical and disciplinary aspects of the Church's life. "Leaving the Church" often means simply trying to function as a Christian without any further reference to, or regard for, the local chancery office or the local parish.

217

There are, of course, various levels of Christian missionary activity. There can be no precise uniformity. Pluralism and flexibility are certainly compatible with the mission which Christ gave directly to every member of the Church (Constitution on the Church, n. 33). But for those who still believe in Jesus as Lord, leaving the Church as such is not a real option. Instead, it may be a question of modifying one's relationship with certain traditional ecclesiastical patterns of life and work.

Q. *This idea of ordaining women to the ministry is in the news again and again these days. The American Lutheran Church, at its annual convention in San Antonio, just voted 560-414 to approve the ordination of women to the ministry. This is the seventh major American denomination to do so. Am I to assume that we Catholics will eventually follow this new trend?*

A. I cannot predict the exact year when the Catholic Church will accept women as candidates for priestly ordination, but I do predict it will happen eventually.

The New Testament does not address itself directly to the problem. Accordingly, there is nothing in the New Testament which speaks decisively against it. Father Edward Schillebeeckx, in a recent article on the theology of the priesthood in *Theology Digest* (summer, 1970), suggests that the early Church began to anticipate the emancipation of women, especially in Hellenistic communities ("There is neither Jew nor Greek, there is neither slave nor free, there is neither male nor female; for you are all one in Christ Jesus"—Gal. 3:28).

Although the ordination of women raises some real problems for the Church, there is no overriding theological argument against the practice. Indeed, the reluctance of many churches to adopt this new practice springs from ecumenical rather than theological, biblical, or doctrinal reasons. These churches do not want to jeopardize the new spirit of fellowship which has emerged in recent years. Of course, as more and more churches accept the ordination of women, the less reason there will be for reluctance on ecumenical grounds.

The Second Vatican Council said nothing about the question, although it did argue on behalf of equality of rights for women (e.g., in the Pastoral Constitution on the Church in the Modern World, n. 29).

Q. *What answer can be given to a person who does not believe in "institutional religion" because he believes it to be a strictly personal issue?*

A. People who think this way usually misunderstand the meaning of "institution." They equate it exclusively with real estate, chancery offices, ecclesiastical law, and so forth. Over against this "institutionalized" religion, they say that they want a simpler, more personal expression of faith. This often includes some form of fellowship, expressed in meetings, common prayer, and liturgy. But each of these is an institutional expression of religion. Indeed, any external, social expression of religious faith is institutional.

When Harvey Cox was criticized for certain anti-institutional leanings in his best-selling book, *The Secular City* (Macmillan, 1965), he responded: "I realize that the church is not pure spirit and cannot live in the modern world, or in any world for that matter, without some institutional expression. Nor is 'institution' just a necessary evil. Institutions, as Arnold Gehlen has shown in his studies of the subject, serve to liberate man rather than to imprison him. Institution is for man what instinct is for animal. Institutions make it possible for the organism to deal with certain levels of decisions by answering a whole range of questions before they are asked . . . . What we need now is a willingness to *reinstitutionalize* the forms of church life based on a conscious theological recognition of what the church's purpose is" (*The Secular City Debate*, D. Callahan, ed., Macmillan, 1966, pp. 186-7).

A religion that is totally deinstitutionalized would have to be a religion with only one adherent, and even then it would be difficult for that individual to avoid institutional expression completely. This is a sociological, and not only a theological, principle.

Indeed, the best "answer" to someone of this anti-institutional cast of mind is to provide some direction for further study in the sociology of religion. The bibliography is long and sometimes highly technical, but there are several basic, introductory texts available, e.g., Thomas F. O'Dea's *The Sociology of Religion* (Prentice-Hall, 1966), Roland Robertson's *The Sociological Interpretation of Religion* (Schocken Books, 1970), and Peter Berger's *The Sacred Canopy: Elements of a Sociological Theory of Religion* (Doubleday, 1967).

For several reasons there has always been an underlying suspicion of sociology among some American Catholics. However, the Second Vatican Council commended its use: "In pastoral care, appropriate use must be made not only of theological principles, but also of the findings of the secular sciences, especially of psychology and sociology. Thus the faithful can be brought to live the faith in a more thorough and mature way" (Pastoral Constitution on the Church in the Modern World, n. 62).

Q. I have often heard it said that Catholics and Lutherans differ on their understanding of the priesthood because we Catholics believe that the power of the priesthood comes from God while the Lutherans believe that it comes from men. Recently, however, I read of the extraordinary agreement reached by Catholic and Lutheran theologians on this same question. Now I'm really confused. Have we Catholics repudiated our earlier views?

A. I am sure you heard correctly. Many Catholics did, in fact, say that one of the major differences between Catholics and Lutherans (or any Protestant, for that matter) concerns the origin of priestly or ministerial power. We Catholics insist it comes from God, while the Lutheran presumably thinks it comes from men. Occasionally you will see this view expressed in print, even today.

There is no justification for it, however. First, it grossly oversimplifies the complexities of theology and doctrine, on both sides; and, secondly, it tends to be unfair, if not insulting, to the faith of non-Catholic Christians.

The recent agreement reached by the Lutheran-Roman Catholic dialogue committee, sponsored jointly by the Bishops' Committee for Ecumenical and Interreligious Affairs and by the U.S.A. National Committee of the Lutheran World Federation, is encouraging indeed.

The Catholic participants (including a bishop and four distinguished theologians) concluded: "We ask the authorities of the Roman Catholic Church whether the ecumenial urgency flowing from Christ's will for unity may not dictate that the Catholic Church should recognize the validity of the Lutheran ministry and, correspondingly, the presence of the body and blood of Christ in the eucharistic celebrations of the Lutheran Churches."

The Lutheran participants (of equally distinguished calibre) urged the same course of action, on the part of their own ecclesiastical leadership, toward the Roman Catholic Church and its ordained priesthood.

For many Catholics, undoubtedly, this new theological consensus will be difficult to understand. We had been taught for so long to believe that the Roman Catholic Church is the "one, true Church of Christ" and that Catholic priests alone have been commissioned by the Lord to preach the Gospel and celebrate the sacraments, especially the Holy Eucharist.

But prompted by such factors as the ecumenical movement, the renewal of biblical studies, the influence of the liturgical movement, our solidarity in suffering during the Second World War, and so forth, we have come to recognize more clearly that non-Roman Catholic churches are also part of the Body of Christ (see the Dogmatic Constitution on the Church, n. 8 and 15, and the Decree on Ecumenism, n. 3). It had been assumed earlier, even in papal encyclicals (especially *Humani Generis,* 1950), that only Roman Catholics were truly within the Body of Christ. Thus, it followed logically that only Roman Catholic orders were valid.

221

As theologians dwell upon the implications of this conciliar teaching (namely, that the Body of Christ embraces non-Catholic Christians as well as Catholic Christians, even though the degree of participation in the Body may vary from church to church), they are beginning to argue in the following way: If the Lutheran Church (or any other comparable Christian community) is within the Body of Christ, this church shares in the mission of that Body. But how can it fulfill the mission (e.g., of preaching and of worship) if it does not have the ministerial and sacramental wherewithal to fulfill it? Thus, the theologians conclude, to the same extent and degree to which these non-Catholic Christian· churches are engrafted upon the Body of Christ, to that same extent and degree are their sacraments and ministry valid.

I do not suggest that every theologian follows this line of reasoning, and I certainly do not imply that every bishop within the Church would now accept it. Nevertheless, it is the direction of thinking for some of the major theologians within the Catholic Church and it is gaining greater and greater acceptance. That is why we are seeing the kind of ecumenical convergence that has been dramatized most recently in this Roman Catholic-Lutheran dialogue on the ordained ministry and priesthood.

Q. What is the Catholic Church's present teaching on papal infallibility, and why did the pope not teach infallibly rather than authentically on artificial birth control, thus avoiding much of the furor his encyclical subsequently aroused? Also, how and when does a pope decide whether he will speak infallibly or authentically?

A. (1) The Catholic Church's present teaching on papal infallibility is the same as it was when initially promulgated at the First Vatican Council in 1870. The most recent authoritative reaffirmation of that doctrine is contained in the Second Vatican Council's Dogmatic Constitution on the Church (n. 25).

(2) The pope did not make an infallible pronouncement on the morality of contraception, in my judgment, because

the subject matter does not pertain directly to the Gospel, but only indirectly. Catholic theologians have said that, in the light of the teaching of Vatican I, it is a matter of faith *(de fide)* that the Church (and the pope, as head of the Church) is infallible when it defines a truth *contained in the deposit of revelation,* and it is theologically certain that the Church (and the pope) is infallible when it defines a truth *necessarily connected with revelation.* The traditional distinction between what is "of faith" and what is "theologically certain" is this: to deny what is "of faith" is heresy; to deny what is "theologically certain" is a theological "error."

One would first have to establish, in the case of *Humanae Vitae,* that the matter of contraception is "necessarily connected" with revelation. It is clearly not part of the deposit of revelation, in any sense of that expression. There are Catholic theologians today, including myself, who would argue that, even if the pope had so desired, he could not have issued an infallible pronouncement on this question. In any case, the burden of proof would be on those who would argue the opposite side of the issue. They would have to show that the matter is "necessarily connected" with divine revelation.

(3) The pope did teach authentically, i.e., he spoke in his official capacity as head of the college of bishops, but without fulfilling all of the specific conditions for an infallible statement, or without even intending to do so. Not every authentic statement, of course, is an infallible definition. With one exception, no pope has tried to attach the note of infallibility to any of his teachings or pronouncements since the definition of papal infallibility in 1870.

(4) Had the pope attempted to make an infallible pronouncement, the furor, as you call it, would have been far greater and ultimately far more divisive than it actually was.

(5) A pope decides to speak authentically (e.g., in an encyclical letter) whenever, in his judgment, he believes a serious pastoral, doctrinal, or moral issue faces the Church and when he thinks that some guidance from his office would benefit both the unity and the missionary responsibility of the

Church. The theological judgment expressed in these authentic teachings is always fallible, which means it is always subject to error.

(6) A pope decides to speak infallibly only after consultation and study (this is at least a *moral* obligation, even if it is not a *conditio sine qua non*). The purpose of such definitions must always be the preservation of the unity of the Church and the safeguarding of the integrity of divine revelation. In this regard, his infallibility is never personal. It is the same infallibility with which the Church itself has been endowed.

Q. *I am convinced that the most serious troubles in the Catholic Church today, especially in the breakdown of authority and the denial of Catholic doctrine, are the responsibility of the sisters teaching in our schools and catechetical programs. I know because I'm a pastor with long experience. My heart goes out to the parents who come complaining to me about what their children are being taught right here in our own backyard. When you protest to higher authorities, they shrug and say, "What can we do?" I wish the pope would publish an encyclical on the mess in religious life and put an end, once and for all, to this chaos.*

A. There are two judgments about sisters which have been making the rounds these past few years: (1) that sisters today are so far ahead of the clergy in theological education and pastoral creativity that the torch of real leadership has now been passed from the hands of the latter to the hands of the former; and (2) that sisters today are so theologically naive, pastorally inept, and psychologically immature that the Church would be better off if sisters were put under wraps (literally as well as figuratively).

Neither judgment can be proved, and neither is really constructive. I have had contact with too many priests in too many dioceses across the United States and Canada to accept the pejorative implications of the first opinion. The clergy (and if it is a minority, it is a solid minority) is composed of men of all ages, temperaments, and backgrounds who have,

224

nonetheless, a common faith in Jesus Christ, a common concern for the Church, and a common commitment to the full realization of the Gospel among men. It would be both senseless and irresponsible to suggest that these men are inherently inferior to some other group within the Church.

Although my professional and pastoral contact with religious communities of women has been less extensive than my association with the diocesan clergy, I should have to conclude that the opinions expressed nowadays by so many Catholics, priests included, about these sisters does indeed border on the ridiculous, at best, and the slanderous, at worst. If we have any reasons at all to have hope in the future of the Church in North America, one very important reason is the idealism, competence, creativity, and insight displayed again and again, not only by many of the so-called rank-and-file among religious women but especially by a significant portion of their leadership.

The "higher authorities" to whom you refer in your letter ought not to shrug their shoulders and adopt a kind of laissez-faire attitude. Bishops and pastors, at every level, have a distinctive ministry to offer to the whole Church, and that is the service of leadership.

I do not mean leadership in the sense of domination or authoritarianism, as it has often been understood in the past. I mean leadership in the sense in which it is described in contemporary theology, sociology, and psychology, on the one hand, and even in the official documents of the Church, on the other (e.g., the November, 1969, pastoral letter of the United States Catholic Bishops on celibacy and the Second Vatican Council's Decree on the Bishops' Pastoral Office in the Church).

"Pastors also know that they themselves were not meant by Christ to shoulder alone the entire saving mission of the Church toward the world. On the contrary, they understand that it is their noble duty so to shepherd the faithful and recognize their services and charismatic gifts that all according to their proper roles may cooperate in this common undertaking with one heart" (Dogmatic Constitution on the Church, n. 30).

Leadership is exercised through coordination and inspiration. The good leader is the one who can bring the best out of people and who can make their distinctive talents work for the common good (see, for example, the Decree on Bishops, n. 13 and 17).

Finally, we should not place too much emphasis on papal encyclicals as a means of "putting to an end" all discussion and debate about a given issue. We should not forget the lessons of the one or two notable failures during the last few years. Disciplinary decisions and actions are deceptively direct and simple, but they are not usually the most productive responses and solutions in the long run.

Q. Three terms—Church, Kingdom of God, and world— are often used almost interchangeably today, even by the so-called religious professionals (clergy and sisters). It can be rather confusing at times. What differences exist among these three realities or are they, in fact, all the same thing?

A. They are not the same thing although it is always the hope of Christians that all of these realities will converge at the end of time (Dogmatic Constitution on the Church, n. 5, and Pastoral Constitution on the Church in the Modern World, n. 39), i.e., that the world (including the Church) might become the Kingdom of God.

The Church is that part of the world which alone confesses that Jesus of Nazareth is the Lord and which, through preaching, worship, example, and service to mankind, strives to make everyone and everything conform to the will of the Father and thereby enter into the Kingdom of God.

The Church and the world are not the same thing, although they overlap, because there are many people and institutions in the world which do not acknowledge the Lordship of Jesus.

The Church and the Kingdom of God are not the same thing, although we trust that they overlap, because there are many whom God has that the Church does not have, and many whom the Church has that God does not yet have (St. Augustine).

Finally, the Kingdom of God and the world are not the same thing, although they may overlap, because much of the world is still under the power of evil and refuses to submit itself to the sovereignty of God.

Q. *In attending the various ecumenical services held in our local Protestant Churches, I get the feeling we are somewha relinquishing that strong feeling that we are the one, true Church. I have had Protestant associates say to me, "You are getting more and more like us." At the risk of sounding "dogmatic," I thought they were supposed to be getting more like us?*

A. You should not feel isolated in your reaction. Many other Catholics share the same sense of wonder about the ecumenical developments of the last five or six years. The reaction of some, in fact, is one of frustration and hostility in the face of such apparent "Protestantizing" tendencies in the Catholic Church.

There are two very different approaches to the ecumenical movement. The first regards ecumenism as a new and more subtle means of bringing non-Catholics into the Catholic Church. Ecumenism, in the minds of these Catholics, is simply a matter of switching from vinegar to honey. But the ultimate goal is the same: the "return" of the Protestant to the Catholic Church.

A second approach to ecumenism rejects the notion of a "return" to Catholic unity and supports instead the idea of a "restoration" of Christian unity. The purpose of the ecumenical movement, in the second view, is to bring the various Christian churches together by encouraging mutual study and mutual respect, on the one hand, and collaboration in Christian mission, on the other (see, for example, the Decree on Ecumenism, n. 4 and 12).

It would appear that the Second Vatican Council favored the rhetoric of "restoration" rather than of "return" (n. 1). Without relinquishing its distinctively Catholic convictions, the council urges Catholics to "joyfully acknowledge and esteem the truly Christian endowments from our common heritage which are to be found among our separated brethren . . . . . Nor should we forget that whatever is wrought by the grace of the Holy Spirit in the hearts of our separated brethren can contribute to our own edification" (n. 4).

The ecumenical movement requires a coming together, not toward one or another fixed expression of the Body of Christ but toward a common, living affirmation of the Gospel of Jesus Christ. It is our prayer that as each community deepens its faithfulness to the one Lord of all mankind, the Spirit will restore to us that precious unity which, through the sin of all parties concerned, was lost so many years ago.

Q. *With all the changes that have taken place in our thinking in the last several years, is it true that we no longer regard the missions as an important aspect of the Church's work?*

A. Not at all. There has been no theological or doctrinal development during the last several years which has eliminated "the missions" from the list of the Church's priorities.

If we believe in the Lordship of Jesus, i.e., that he is "the goal of human history, the focal point of the belongings of history and of civilization, the center of the human race, the joy of every heart, and the answer to all its yearnings" (Pastoral Constitution on the Church in the Modern World, n. 45), then this is a perception which we are bound to share with others (Constitution on the Church, n. 17).

There may have been some Catholics in past years who tended to equate "the missions" of the Church with the very *mission* of the Church. This would be theologically inaccurate.

To the extent that we have broadened our understanding of the mission of the Church to include more than "the missions," there has been a change in our thinking about the missionary apostolate. However, such a change has not diminished the importance of preaching the Gospel to those

228

who do not yet believe in Christ. Rather, it has provided such activity with a wider theological foundation.

It is instructive to note the difference in orientation between the council's Decree on the Church's Missionary Activity, on the one hand, and its Dogmatic Constitution on the Church and its Pastoral Constitution on the Church in the Modern World, on the other.

The tendency in the former document is to continue the identification of "the missions" with the *mission* of the Church: "The specific purpose of this missionary activity is evangelization and the planting of the Church among those peoples and groups where she has not yet taken root" (n. 6).

The perspective employed in the Dogmatic Constitution on the Church and in the Pastoral Constitution seems closer to the insights of recent and contemporary ecclesiology.

Lumen Gentium refers to the Church as a sacrament of Christ, or "sign of intimate union with God, and of the unity of all mankind. She is also the instrument for the achievement of such union and unity" (n. 1). Furthermore, the Church exists to continue the work of Jesus for the sake of the Kingdom: to proclaim it, to embody it, and to establish it among the nations (n. 5). The document does not identify the Church with that Kingdom, but refers to the Church instead as the "initial budding forth" of God's reign among men.

The Pastoral Constitution declares that the Church exists to foster "that brotherhood of all men which corresponds to this destiny of theirs" (n. 3). Thus, the Church exists to carry on the ministry of Jesus "to give witness to the truth,—to rescue and not sit in judgment, to serve and not to be served."

"By virtue of her mission to shed on the whole world the radiance of the gospel message, and to unify under one Spirit all men of whatever nation, race, or culture, the Church stands forth as a sign of that brotherliness which allows honest dialogue and invigorates it" (n. 92).

The Church continues to have a responsibility for the non-evangelized, with the hope of bringing them, under God's grace, to faith in Jesus as the Christ. But that is one principal aspect of its larger, multiple responsibility for the coming of God's Kingdom among all mankind (n. 45).

Q. *Suppose some historian were able to prove, beyond all reasonable doubt, that one of the popes in centuries gone by was invalidly elected and consecrated. Would not such a finding completely undermine the claims of the Catholic Church to be the one Church having legitimate apostolic succession?*

A. No. Apostolic succession does not mean chronological continuity. What do I mean here by "chronological continuity"?

Many Catholics continue to think that the Catholic Church is "the one true Church of Christ" because it can trace its teachings and sacramental authority (conferred in Holy Order) all the way back, in an unbroken line, to the time of Christ and the Apostles.

In this view, the basis of our claims regarding apostolicity is our ability to show that the pope and the bishops of the Catholic Church today enjoy the very same authority and power which the first Apostles enjoyed and which they, in turn, intended to pass along, in an unbroken chain, to every succeeding generation.

Thus, the present college of bishops are said to be the successors of the Apostles, enjoying the same place and prerogatives as the original Twelve enjoyed.

Indeed, there is something of this notion of apostolic succession in the third chapter of the Dogmatic Constitution on the Church (e.g., n. 22).

Such an understanding of apostolic succession, however, cannot easily be reconciled with recent biblical and theological scholarship. See, for example, Father Raymond B. Brown's *Priest and Bishop: Biblical Reflections* (Paulist Press, 1971) and Hans Küng's *Structures of the Church* (Nelson, 1964), pp. 172-89, and *The Church* (Sheed & Ward, 1967), pp. 344-59.

Apostolic succession applies in the first instance to the whole Church. It means that every Christian has the responsibility to continue the work which the Apostles themselves exercised by the will and commission of Jesus Christ.

The Apostles, like Jesus, were to carry on his work of proclaiming the Kingdom of God, of giving praise and thanksgiving to the Father, of offering themselves and their communities as signs or sacraments of God's presence among men, and of using whatever resources they had for the sake of those in need (see the Dogmatic Constitution on the Church, n. 5).

This apostolic mission remains the mission of the People of God today (see chapter II of the same Constitution) and what is said in this regard of the People of God applies equally to laity, religious, and clergy alike (n. 30), for indeed the lay apostolate is a participation in the saving mission of the Church itself and not merely a sharing in the ministry of the hierarchy (n. 33).

"Perhaps as a result of a better historical understanding of why there are difficulties, Catholics shall be able to modify an often too simplistic concept of the bishops as the successors of the apostles and in so doing enable the bishops to serve more effectively and realistically as the formal representatives of an apostolic succession that must be shared more broadly" (R. Brown, *Priest and Bishop*, p. 81).

Q. Doesn't theology always have to be subjected to the authority of revelation? When there are different theological opinions about some important issue, doesn't the Church have the right and the duty to measure such opinions against the objective truth of revelation itself?

A. All things, including theology, are subject to the Word of God (see, for example, the Dogmatic Constitution on Divine Revelation, n. 25). No one disagrees with that principle.

The problem is that the determination of the nature and content of revelation, or of God's Word, is itself a matter of interpretation.

Revelation exists nowhere in a pure, untheological form, not even in the Bible. The Bible itself is an interpretation of history. The New Testament, in particular, is an interpretation of history in the light of Jesus, whom it perceives to be the Lord of history. Biblical theology, therefore, is really an interpretation of an interpretation.

In other words, it is impossible to grasp God's Word in the raw, so to speak. The Word of God exists nowhere in a condition which is completely free of interpretation. And since the interpretation of God's Word is what theology is all about, we might justifiably say that revelation, or the Word of God, can never be measured except theologically.

Consequently, to suggest that theology can somehow be judged by revelation in a purely objective, *non*-theological way, really makes no sense. The very determination of the meaning and content of revelation is itself a theological task.

The practical question, therefore, is this: *Which theology* are you using to refute another theology *in the name of God's Word?*

Q. Earlier you discussed the question of parish and diocesan councils. If, as you reported, there is "no biblical, doctrinal, or theological reason" for regarding such bodies as merely advisory, what structures now exist which can prevent the bishop or the pastor from simply vetoing a proposal endorsed by the majority of such councils? Or aren't we supposed to imagine that such problems can arise in a community protected by the Holy Spirit?

A. The distinctive leadership role of the bishop or pastor can be protected by the power of veto, but it seems to me that the council ought to be able to override such a veto by a reasonable majority, e.g., two-thirds or three-quarters. If such vetoes can never be overridden, under any circumstances, then we are right back where we started, with the bishop or pastor functioning, for all practical purposes, as a kind of absolute monarch.

The point of these remarks can easily be misunderstood. It may appear that our primary concern today is to strip bishops and pastors of their power. On the contrary, our principal concern is to fulfill the theological and pastoral designs of the Second Vatican Council; namely, to incorporate the whole People of God into the decision-making process of Church life and mission, for which every member of the Church—laity, religious, and clergy alike—are responsible (Dogmatic Constitution on the Church, n. 30 and 33).

Q. If two Catholics marry outside the Catholic Church and in opposition to the laws of the Church, why should their children be punished? We can understand why we are forbidden to receive Holy Communion, but why should the same law apply to our children, who are totally innocent in this matter?

A. There is no reason why the children of a canonically invalid marriage should be denied the sacraments unless there is no realistic hope that these children will persist in their baptismal vocation and be faithful, as far as possible, to the mission of the Church.

Furthermore, you should not totally and absolutely discount the possibility of your own return, if only occasionally, to the sacraments, even when there is no possibility of rectifying your situation. It was once uncritically assumed that Catholics who are involved in a canonically invalid marriage could never, under any circumstances (except danger of death, with an expression of contrition), receive Holy Communion. Whereas this may still be a general norm, it is not so absolute that it can admit of no exceptions. You should consult with a priest in whom you have some confidence.

I realize that this answer, so brief and cryptic, may create confusion in the minds of some readers (and headaches for a few priests), but there are very many Catholics who still think that Catholics who are involved in an invalid marriage are forever prevented from receiving the sacraments, unless of course they wish to correct their situation (which means, in many cases, leaving their partner in marriage).

This rigid approach is subject to challenge, and people have a right to know it.

233

Readers, especially parish priests, may consult the extended study of the Canon Law Society of America, "Intolerable Marriage Situations: Conflict Between External and Internal Forum," *The Jurist*, 1970: 1.

Q. As a Protestant reader of your work, I have been impressed with the many positive things you have been able to say about Christians such as myself. I realize that this is part of a new mood and attitude of many Catholics, but is it something endorsed by your Church's leaders? Do you think that we'll ever get together again? How will such a reunited Church look?

A. Ecumenism is both a movement and a state of mind. As a movement it can be defined as the sum total of "those activities and enterprises which, according to various needs of the Church and opportune occasions, are started and organized for the fostering of unity among Christians" (Decree on Ecumenism, Second Vatican Council, n. 4).

As a state of mind, ecumenism is an attitude of openness towards Christians of different traditions in order to learn from their distinctive experiences and example and in order to purify and deepen our own commitment to the Gospel of Jesus Christ.

"There can be no ecumenism worthy of the name without a change of heart," the Decree on Ecumenism continues (n. 7). "For it is from newness of attitudes, from self-denial and unstinted love, that yearnings for unity take their rise and grow toward maturity. We should therefore pray to the divine Spirit for the grace to be genuinely self-denying, humble, gentle in the service of others, and to have an attitude of brotherly generosity toward them."

Ecumenism, both as a movement and as a state of mind, has been endorsed many times by the official leadership of the Church. The Decree on Ecumenism is, of course, the most important document on this question.

Will we ever get together again? It is difficult to improve upon the concluding remarks of this same Decree on Ecumenism: "This most sacred Synod urgently desires that the initiatives of the sons of the Catholic Church, joined with those of the separated brethren, go forward without obstructing the ways of divine Providence and without prejudicing the future inspiration of the Holy Spirit. Further, this Synod declares its realization that the holy task of reconciling all Christians in the unity of the one and only Church of Christ transcends human energies and abilities. It therefore places its hope entirely in the prayer of Christ for the Church, in the love of the Father for us, and in the power of the Holy Spirit" (n. 24).

To my knowledge no one has as yet devised a precise blueprint for the united Church of the future. Oftentimes, however, Christians of various traditions assume that the reunited Church of the future must somehow look like their own churches do even today. This is especially true of many Catholics, who think that reunion means that all non-Catholic Christians accept the authority of the pope, the Code of Canon Law, the seven sacraments, the compendium of Catholic doctrinal formulations, and so forth, in exactly the sense in which these realities are presently understood and/or exercised.

In other words, there are many Christians, Catholics included, who confuse unity with uniformity. However, the Decree on Ecumenism reminds us that such an identification is unnecessary and may even be harmful to the future of the ecumenical movement: "While preserving unity in essentials, let all members of the Church, according to the office entrusted to each, preserve a proper freedom in the various forms of spiritual life and discipline, in the variety of liturgical rites, and even in the theological elaborations of revealed truth" (n. 4).

On that last point, the decree also stated: "When comparing doctrines, they should remember that in Catholic teaching there exists an order or 'hierarchy' of truths, since they vary in their relationship to the foundation of the Christian faith" (n. 11).

Thus, it is certainly necessary for unity that all Christians accept Jesus of Nazareth as Lord, but it is of far less importance—and not essential for unity—that all Christians believe in the existence of angels or that Mary is the mediatrix of all grace.

APPENDIX II

SUGGESTED READINGS

1. If you were helped by the presentations contained in this book, you might wish to consult some of the other material that I have produced in the recent past: *Do We Need the Church?* (New York: Harper & Row, 1969) and *Church: The Continuing Quest* (New York: Newman Press, 1970), both of which offer a systematic discussion of the mission of the Church, and *What Do We Really Believe?* (Dayton: Pflaum Press, 1969), which is a discussion book similar to this one, but whose range of interest is even wider: from the problem of God to the problem of the Second Coming.

2. The most accessible scholarly material on the theology of the Church is Hans Küng's *The Church* (New York: Sheed & Ward, 1967) and his earlier work, *Structures of the Church* (New York: Nelson, 1964). Both books deal extensively with the question of ecclesiastical office, papacy, collegiality, and so forth, all of which are of particular relevance to the question, "Who is a Catholic?"

3. At a more popular, but no less useful, level are some recent books by Gregory Baum, *The Credibility of the Church Today: A Reply to Charles Davis* (New York: Herder & Herder, 1968) and *Faith and Doctrine: A Contemporary View* (New York: Newman Press, 1969). Each of these volumes directly

237

confronts the question, "Why be a Catholic?" and each attempts an essentially positive response.

4. Important questions such as papal infallibility, the development of dogma, and the place of the ordained ministry in the Church are treated in such recent works as Hans Küng's *Infallible? An Inquiry* (New York: Doubleday, 1971), Avery Dulles' *The Survival of Dogma* (New York: Doubleday, 1971), and Raymond Brown's *Priest and Bishop: Biblical Reflections* (New York: Paulist Press, 1971).

5. A quasi-popular exposition and explanation of the Roman Catholic experience is available in John McKenzie's *The Roman Catholic Church* (New York: Holt, Rinehart and Winston, 1969).

6. George Lindbeck offers one of the most sympathetic Protestant discussions of Catholic thought and practice in his *The Future of Roman Catholic Theology* (Philadelphia: Fortress Press, 1970).

7. Compact, scholarly treatments of individual topics related to the problem of the Church in general and Catholicism in particular are available in *Sacramentum Mundi: An Encyclopedia of Theology*, 6 vols. (New York: Herder & Herder 1968-1970).

Are there any questions about Catholicism which this book does not adequately consider? Which issues relative to the topic of this book do you think theologians should address themselves to more fully in the months and years ahead? Send your suggestions to me, care of the publisher.

INDEX OF NAMES

INDEX OF TOPICS

241

INDEX